The Tragedy of Valentinian by John Fletcher

John Fletcher was born in December, 1579 in Rye, Sussex. He was baptised on December 20th.

As can be imagined details of much of his life and career have not survived and, accordingly, only a very brief indication of his life and works can be given.

Young Fletcher appears at the very young age of eleven to have entered Corpus Christi College at Cambridge University in 1591. There are no records that he ever took a degree but there is some small evidence that he was being prepared for a career in the church.

However what is clear is that this was soon abandoned as he joined the stream of people who would leave University and decamp to the more bohemian life of commercial theatre in London.

The upbringing of the now teenage Fletcher and his seven siblings now passed to his paternal uncle, the poet and minor official Giles Fletcher. Giles, who had the patronage of the Earl of Essex may have been a liability rather than an advantage to the young Fletcher. With Essex involved in the failed rebellion against Elizabeth Giles was also tainted.

By 1606 John Fletcher appears to have equipped himself with the talents to become a playwright. Initially this appears to have been for the Children of the Queen's Revels, then performing at the Blackfriars Theatre.

Fletcher's early career was marked by one significant failure; The Faithful Shepherdess, his adaptation of Giovanni Battista Guarini's Il Pastor Fido, which was performed by the Blackfriars Children in 1608.

By 1609, however, he had found his stride. With his collaborator John Beaumont, he wrote Philaster, which became a hit for the King's Men and began a profitable association between Fletcher and that company. Philaster appears also to have begun a trend for tragicomedy.

By the middle of the 1610s, Fletcher's plays had achieved a popularity that rivalled Shakespeare's and cemented the pre-eminence of the King's Men in Jacobean London. After his frequent early collaborator John Beaumont's early death in 1616, Fletcher continued working, both singly and in collaboration, until his own death in 1625. By that time, he had produced, or had been credited with, close to fifty plays.

Index of contents

DRAMATIS PERSONAE
THE SCENE: Rome.
ACTUS PRIMUS
SCÆNA PRIMA
SCÆNA SECUNDA
SCÆNA TERTIA
ACTUS SECUNDUS
SCÆNA PRIMA
SCÆNA SECUNDA

SCÆNA TERTIA
SCÆNA QUARTA
ACTUS TERTIUS
SCÆNA PRIMA
SCÆNA SECUNDA
SCÆNA TERTIA
ACTUS QUARTUS
SCÆNA PRIMA
SCÆNA SECUNDA
SCÆNA TERTIA
SCÆNA QUARTA
ACTUS QUINTUS
SCÆNA PRIMA
SCÆNA SECUNDA
SCÆNA TERTIA
SCÆNA QUARTA
SCÆNA QUINTA
SCÆNA SEXTA
SCÆNA SEPTIMA
SCÆNA OCTAVIA
EPILOGUE
JOHN FLETCHER – A SHORT BIOGRAPHY
JOHN FLETCHER – A CONCISE BIBLIOGRAPHY

DRAMATIS PERSONAE
MAN
Valentinian, Emperour of Rome.
Æcius, the Emperours Loyal General.
Balbus   }
Proculus   } 4 Noble Panders, and flatterers
Chilax   } to the Emperour.
Licinius   }
Maximus, a great Souldier, Husband to Lucina.
Lycias, an Eunuch.
Pontius, an honest Cashier'd Centurion.
Phidias } two bold and faithful Eunuchs,
Aretus } Servants to Æcius.
Afranius, an eminent Captain.
Paulus, a Poet.
Licippus, a Courtier.
3 Senators.
Physicians.
Gentlemen.
Souldiers.
WOMEN
Eudoxia, Empress, Wife to Valentinian.

Lucina, the chast abused Wife of Maximus.
Claudia   } Lucina's waiting Women.
Marcellina   }
Ardelia } two of the Emperours
Phorba } Bawds.

THE SCENE: Rome.

ACTUS PRIMUS

SCÆNA PRIMA

Enter **BALBUS, PROCULUS, CHILAX, LICINIUS.**

BALBUS
I Never saw the like, she's no more stirr'd,
No more another Woman, no more alter'd
With any hopes or promises laid to her
(Let 'em be ne're so weighty, ne're so winning)
Than I am with the motion of mine own legs.

PROCULUS
Chilax,
You are a stranger yet in these designs,
At least in Rome; tell me, and tell me truth,
Did you ere know in all your course of practice,
In all the wayes of Women you have run through
(For I presume you have been brought up Chilax,
As we to fetch and carry.)

CHILAX
True I have so.

PROCULUS
Did you I say again in all this progress,
Ever discover such a piece of beauty,
Ever so rare a Creature, and no doubt
One that must know her worth too, and affect it,
I and be flatter'd, else 'tis none: and honest?
Honest against the tide of all temptations,
Honest to one man, to her Husband only,
And yet not eighteen, not of age to know
Why she is honest?

CHILAX
I confess it freely,
I never saw her fellow, nor e're shall,
For all our Grecian Dames, all I have tri'd,
(And sure I have tri'd a hundred, if I say two
I speak within my compass) all these beauties,
And all the constancy of all these faces,
Maids, Widows, Wives, of what degree or calling,
So they be Greeks, and fat, for there's my cunning,
I would undertake and not sweat for't, Proculus,
Were they to try again, say twice as many,
Under a thousand pound, to lay 'em bedrid;
But this Wench staggers me.

LICINIUS
Do you see these Jewels?
You would think these pretty baits; now I'le assure ye
Here's half the wealth of Asia.

BALBUS
These are nothing
To the full honours I propounded to her;
I bid her think, and be, and presently
What ever her ambition, what the Counsel
Of others would add to her, what her dreams
Could more enlarge, what any President
Of any Woman rising up to glory,
And standing certain there, and in the highest,
Could give her more, nay to be Empress.

PROCULUS
And cold at all these offers?

BALBUS
Cold as Crystal,
Never to be thaw'd again.

CHILAX
I tri'd her further,
And so far, that I think she is no Woman,
At least as Women go now.

LICINIUS
Why what did you?

CHILAX
I offered that, that had she been but Mistris
Of as much spleen as Doves have, I had reach'd her;

A safe revenge of all that ever hates her,
The crying down for ever of all beauties
That may be thought come near her.

PROCULUS
That was pretty.

CHILAX
I never knew that way fail, yet I'le tell ye
I offer'd her a gift beyond all yours,
That, that had made a Saint start, well consider'd,
The Law to be her creature, she to make it,
Her mouth to give it, every creature living
From her aspect, to draw their good or evil
Fix'd in 'em spight of Fortune; a new Nature
She should be called, and Mother of all ages,
Time should be hers, and what she did, lame vertue
Should bless to all posterities: her Air
Should give us life, her earth and water feed us.
And last, to none but to the Emperour,
(And then but when she pleas'd to have it so)
She should be held for mortal.

LICINIUS
And she heard you?

CHILAX
Yes, as a Sick man hears a noise, or he
That stands condemn'd his judgment, let me perish,
But if there can be vertue, if that name
Be any thing but name and empty title,
If it be so as fools have been pleas'd to feign it,
A power that can preserve us after ashes,
And make the names of men out-reckon ages,
This Woman has a God of vertue in her.

BALBUS
I would the Emperor were that God.

CHILAX
She has in her
All the contempt of glory and vain seeming
Of all the Stoicks, all the truth of Christians,
And all their Constancy: Modesty was made
When she was first intended: when she blushes
It is the holiest thing to look upon;
The purest temple of her sect, that ever
Made Nature a blest Founder.

PROCULUS
Is there no way
To take this Phenix?

LICINIUS
None but in her ashes.

CHILAX
If she were fat, or any way inclining
To ease or pleasure, or affected glory,
Proud to be seen and worship'd, 'twere a venture;
But on my soul she is chaster than cold Camphire.

BALBUS
I think so too; for all the waies of Woman,
Like a full sail she bears against: I askt her
After my many offers walking with her,
And her as many down-denyals, how
If the Emperour grown mad with love should force her;
She pointed to a Lucrece, that hung by,
And with an angry look, that from her eyes
Shot Vestal fire against me, she departed.

PROCULUS
This is the first wench I was ever pos'd in,
Yet I have brought young loving things together
This two and thirty years.

CHILAX
I find by this wench
The calling of a Bawd to be a strange,
A wise, and subtile calling; and for none
But staid, discreet, and understanding people:
And as the Tutor to great Alexander,
Would say, a young man should not dare to read
His moral books, till after five and twenty;
So must that he or she, that will be bawdy,
(I mean discreetly bawdy, and be trusted)
If they will rise, and gain experience,
Well steept in years, and discipline, begin it,
I take it 'tis no Boys play.

BALBUS
Well, what's thought of?

PROCULUS
The Emperour must know it.

LICINIUS
If the woman should chance to fail too.

CHILAX
As 'tis ten to one.

PROCULUS
Why what remains, but new nets for the purchase?

CHILAX
Let's go consider then: and if all fail,
This is the first quick Eele, that sav'd her tail.

[Exeunt.

SCÆNA SECUNDA

Enter **LUCINA**, **ARDELIA** and **PHORBA**.

ARDELIA
You still insist upon that Idol, Honour,
Can it renew your youth, can it add wealth,
That takes off wrinkles: can it draw mens eyes,
To gaze upon you in your age? can honour,
That truly is a Saint to none but Souldiers,
And look'd into, bears no reward but danger,
Leave you the most respected person living?
Or can the common kisses of a Husband,
(Which to a sprightly Lady is a labour)
Make ye almost Immortal? ye are cozen'd,
The honour of a woman is her praises;
The way to get these, to be seen, and sought too,
And not to bury such a happy sweetness
Under a smoaky roof.

LUCINA
I'le hear no more.

PHORBA
That white, and red, and all that blessed beauty,
Kept from the eyes, that make it so, is nothing;
Then you are rarely fair, when men proclaim it;
The Phenix, were she never seen, were doubted;
That most unvalued Horn the Unicorn
Bears to oppose the Huntsman, were it nothing

But tale, and meer tradition, would help no man;
But when the vertue's known, the honour's doubled:
Vertue is either lame, or not at all,
And love a Sacriledge, and not a Saint,
When it bars up the way to mens Petitions.

ARDELIA
Nay ye shall love your Husband too; we come not
To make a Monster of ye.

LUCINA
Are ye women?

ARDELIA
You'll find us so, and women you shall thank too,
If you have grace to make your use.

LUCINA
Fye on ye.

PHORBA
Alas poor bashful Lady, by my soul,
Had ye no other vertue, but your blushes,
And I a man, I should run mad for those:
How daintily they set her off, how sweetly!

ARDELIA
Come Goddess, come, you move too near the earth,
It must not be, a better Orb stayes for you:
Here: be a Maid, and take 'em.

LUCINA
Pray leave me.

PHORBA
That were a sin sweet Lady, and a way
To make us guilty of your melancholy:
You must not be alone; in conversation
Doubts are resolv'd, and what sticks near the conscience
Made easie, and allowable.

LUCINA
Ye are Devils.

ARDELIA
That you may one day bless for your damnation.

LUCINA

I charge ye in the name of Chastity,
Tempt me no more; how ugly ye seem to me?
There is no wonder men defame our Sex,
And lay the vices of all ages on us,
When such as you shall bear the names of women;
If ye had eyes to see your selves, or sence
Above the base rewards ye play the bawds for:
If ever in your lives ye heard of goodness,
(Though many Regions off, as men hear Thunder)
If ever ye had Mothers, and they souls:
If ever Fathers, and not such as you are;
If ever any thing were constant in you,
Besides your sins, or coming, but your courses;
If ever any of your Ancestors
Dyed worth a noble deed, that would be cherish'd;
Soul-frighted with this black infection,
You would run from one another, to repentance,
And from your guilty eyes drop out those sins,
That made ye blind, and beasts.

PHORBA
Ye speak well, Lady;
A sign of fruitful education,
If your religious zeal had wisdom with it.

ARDELIA
This Lady was ordain'd to bless the Empire,
And we may all give thanks for't.

PHORBA
I believe ye.

ARDELIA
If any thing redeem the Emperour
From his wild flying courses, this is she;
She can instruct him if ye mark; she is wise too.

PHORBA
Exceeding wise, which is a wonder in her,
And so religious, that I well believe,
Though she would sin she cannot.

ARDELIA
And besides,
She has the Empires cause in hand, not loves;
There lies the main consideration,
For which she is chiefly born.

PHORBA

She finds that point
Stronger than we can tell her, and believe it
I look by her means for a reformation,
And such a one, and such a rare way carried
That all the world shall wonder at.

ARDELIA

'Tis true;
I never thought the Emperor had wisdom,
Pity, or fair affection to his Country,
Till he profest this love: gods give 'em Children,
Such as her vertues merit, and his zeal.
I look to see a Numa from this Lady,
Or greater than Octavius.

PHORBA

Do you mark too,
Which is a Noble vertue, how she blushes,
And what a flowing modesty runs through her,
When we but name the Emperour?

ARDELIA

But mark it,
Yes, and admire it too, for she considers,
Though she be fair as Heaven, and vertuous
As holy truth, yet to the Emperour
She is a kind of nothing but her service,
Which she is bound to offer, and she'll do it,
And when her Countries cause commands affection,
She knows obedience is the key of vertues,
Then flye the blushes out like Cupid's arrows,
And though the tye of Marriage to her Lord
Would fain cry, stay Lucina, yet the cause
And general wisdom of the Princes love,
Makes her find surer ends and happier,
And if the first were chaste, this is twice doubled.

PHORBA

Her tartness unto us too.

ARDELIA

That's a wise one.

PHORBA

I rarely like, it shews a rising wisdom,
That chides all common fools as dare enquire
What Princes would have private.

ARDELIA
What a Lady
Shall we be blest to serve?

LUCINA
Go get ye from me:
Ye are your purses Agents, not the Princes:
Is this the vertuous Lore ye train'd me out to?
Am I a woman fit to imp your vices?
But that I had a Mother, and a woman
Whose ever living fame turns all it touches,
Into the good it self is, I should now
Even doubt my self, I have been search't so near
The very soul of honour: why should you two,
That happily have been as chaste as I am,
Fairer, I think, by much, for yet your faces,
Like ancient well built piles, shew worthy ruins,
After that Angel age, turn mortal Devils?
For shame, for woman-hood, for what ye have been,
For rotten Cedars have born goodly branches,
If ye have hope of any Heaven, but Court,
Which like a Dream, you'l find hereafter vanish,
Or at the best but subject to repentance,
Study no more to be ill spoken of;
Let women live themselves, if they must fall,
Their own destruction find 'em, not your Fevours.

ARDELIA
Madam, ye are so excellent in all,
And I must tell it you with admiration,
So true a joy ye have, so sweet a fear,
And when ye come to anger, 'tis so noble,
That for mine own part, I could still offend,
To hear you angry; women that want that,
And your way guided (else I count it nothing)
Are either Fools, or Cowards.

PHORBA
She were a Mistris for no private greatness,
Could she not frown a ravish'd kiss from anger,
And such an anger as this Lady learns us,
Stuck with such pleasing dangers. Gods (I ask ye)
Which of ye all could hold from?

LUCINA
I perceive ye,
Your own dark sins dwell with ye, and that price

You sell the chastity of modest wives at
Runs to diseases with your bones: I scorn ye,
And all the nets ye've pitcht to catch my vertues
Like Spiders Webs, I sweep away before me.
Go tell the Emperour, ye have met a woman,
That neither his own person, which is God-like,
The world he rules, nor what that world can purchase,
Nor all the glories subject to a Cæsar,
The honours that he offers for my body,
The hopes, gifts, everlasting flatteries,
Nor any thing that's his, and apt to tempt me,
No not to be the Mother of the Empire,
And Queen of all the holy fires he worships,
Can make a Whore of.

ARDELIA
You mistake us Lady.

LUCINA
Yet tell him this has thus much weaken'd me,
That I have heard his Knaves, and you his Matrons,
Fit Nurses for his sins, which gods forgive me;
But ever to be leaning to his folly,
Or to be brought to love his lust, assure him,
And from her mouth, whose life shall make it certain,
I never can: I have a noble Husband,
Pray tell him that too, yet a noble name,
A Noble Family, and last a Conscience:
Thus much for your answer: For your selves,
Ye have liv'd the shame of women, dye the better.

[Exit **LUCINA**.

PHORBA
What's now to do?

ARDELIA
Ev'n as she said, to dye,
For there's no living here, and women thus,
I am sure for us two.

PHORBA
Nothing stick upon her?

ARDELIA
We have lost a mass of mony; well Dame Vertue,
Yet ye may halt if good luck serve.

PHORBA
Worms take her,
She has almost spoil'd our trade.

ARDELIA
So godly;
This is ill breeding, Phorba.

PHORBA
If the women
Should have a longing now to see this Monster,
And she convert 'em all.

ARDELIA
That may be, Phorba,
But if it be, I'll have the young men gelded;
Come, let's go think, she must not 'scape us thus;
There is a certain season, if we hit,
That women may be rid without a Bit.

[Exeunt.

SCÆNA TERTIA

Enter **MAXIMUS** and **ÆCIUS**.

MAXIMUS
I cannot blame the Nations, noble friend,
That they fall off so fast from this wild man,
When (under our Allegiance be it spoken,
And the most happy tye of our affections)
The worlds weight groans beneath him; Where lives vertue,
Honour, discretion, wisdom? who are call'd
And chosen to the steering of the Empire
But Bawds, and singing Girls? O my Æcius
The glory of a Souldier, and the truth
Of men made up for goodness sake, like shells
Grow to the ragged walls for want of action;
Only your happy self, and I that love you,
Which is a larger means to me than favour.

ÆCIUS
No more, my worthy friend, though these be truths,
And though these truths would ask a Reformation,
At least a little squaring: yet remember,
We are but Subjects, Maximus; obedience

To what is done, and grief for what is ill done,
Is all we can call ours: The hearts of Princes
Are like the Temples of the gods; pure incense,
Until unhallowed hands defile those offerings,
Burns ever there; we must not put 'em out,
Because the Priests that touch those sweets, are wicked;
We dare not, dearest Friend, nay more, we cannot,
While we consider who we are, and how,
To what laws bound, much more to what Law-giver;
Whilest Majesty is made to be obeyed,
And not to be inquired into, whilst gods and angels
Make but a rule as we do, though a stricter;
Like desperate and unseason'd Fools let flye
Our killing angers, and forsake our honours.

MAXIMUS
My noble Friend, from whose instructions
I never yet took surfeit, weigh but thus much,
Nor think I speak it with ambition,
For by the gods, I do not; why Æcius,
Why are we thus, or how become thus wretched?

ÆCIUS
You'll fall again into your fit.

MAXIMUS
I will not;
Or are we now no more the Sons of Romans,
No more the followers of their happy fortunes,
But conquer'd Gauls, or Quivers for the Parthians?
Why, is this Emperour, this man we honour,
This God that ought to be?

ÆCIUS
You are too curious.

MAXIMUS
Good, give me leave, why is this Author of us?

ÆCIUS
I dare not hear ye speak thus.

MAXIMUS
I'll be modest,
Thus led away, thus vainly led away,
And we Beholders? misconceive me not,
I sow no danger in my words; But wherefore,
And to what end, are we the Sons of Fathers

Famous and fast to Rome? why are their Vertues
Stampt in the dangers of a thousand Battels?
For goodness sake, their honours, time outdaring?
I think for our example.

ÆCIUS
Ye speak nobly.

MAXIMUS
Why are we seeds of these then, to shake hands
With Bawds and base informers, kiss discredit,
And court her like a Mistriss? 'pray, your leave yet;
You'll say the Emperour is young, and apt
To take impression rather from his pleasures
Than any constant worthiness, it may be,
But why do these, the people call his pleasures,
Exceed the moderation of a man?
Nay to say justly, friend, why are they vices,
And such as shake our worths with forreign Nations?

ÆCIUS
You search the sore too deep, and I must tell ye,
In any other man this had been boldness,
And so rewarded; 'pray depress your spirit,
For though I constantly believe you honest,
Ye were no friend for me else, and what now
Ye freely spake, but good you owe to th' Empire,
Yet take heed, worthy Maximus, all ears
Hear not with that distinction mine do, few
You'll find admonishers, but urgers of your actions,
And to the heaviest (friend;) and pray consider
We are but shadows, motions others give us,
And though our pities may become the times,
Justly our powers cannot; make me worthy
To be your friend ever in fair Allegiance,
But not in force; For durst mine own soul urge me,
(And by that Soul I speak my just affections)
To turn my hand from Truth, which is obedience,
And give the helm my Vertue holds, to Anger;
Though I had both the Blessings of the Bruti,
And both their instigations, though my Cause
Carried a face of Justice beyond theirs,
And as I am a servant to my fortunes,
That daring soul, that first taught disobedience,
Should feel the first example: say the Prince,
As I may well believe, seems vicious,
Who justly knows 'tis not to try our honours?
Or say he be an ill Prince, are we therefore

Fit fires to purge him? No, my dearest friend,
The Elephant is never won with anger,
Nor must that man that would reclaim a Lion,
Take him by th' teeth.

MAXIMUS
I pray mistake me not.

ÆCIUS
Our honest actions, and the light that breaks
Like morning from our service, chaste and blushing,
Is that that pulls a Prince back; then he sees,
And not till then truly repents his errours,
When Subjects Crystal Souls are glasses to him.

MAXIMUS
My ever honour'd friend, I'll take your counsel.
The Emperour appears, I'll leave ye to him.
And as we both affect him, may he flourish.

[Exit **MAXIMUS**.

[Enter the **EMPEROUR** and **CHILAX**.

EMPEROUR
Is that the best news?

CHILAX
Yet the best we know, Sir.

EMPEROUR
Bid Maximus come to me, and be gone then;
Mine own head be my helper, these are fools:
How now Æcius, are the Souldiers quiet?

ÆCIUS
Better I hope, Sir, than they were.

EMPEROUR
They are pleas'd, I hear,
To censure me extreamly for my pleasures,
Shortly they'll fight against me.

ÆCIUS
Gods defend, Sir.
And for their censures they are such shrew'd Judgers;
A donative of ten Sestertias
I'll undertake shall make 'em ring your praises

More than they sang your pleasures.

EMPEROUR
I believe thee;
Art thou in love, Æcius, yet?

ÆCIUS
O no Sir;
I am too course for Ladies; my embraces,
That only am acquainted with Alarms,
Would break their tender Bodies.

EMPEROUR
Never fear it,
They are stronger than ye think, they'll hold the Hammer.
My Empress swears thou art a lusty Souldier,
A good one I believe thee.

ÆCIUS
All that goodness
Is but your Graces Creature.

EMPEROUR
Tell me truly,
For thou dar'st tell me.

ÆCIUS
Any thing concerns ye,
That's fit for me to speak and you to pardon.

EMPEROUR
What say the Souldiers of me, and the same words,
Mince 'em not, good Æcius, but deliver
The very forms and tongues they talk withal.

ÆCIUS
I'll tell your Grace, but with this caution
You be not stir'd, for should the gods live with us,
Even those we certainly believe are righteous,
Give 'em but drink, they would censure them too.

EMPEROUR
Forward.

ÆCIUS
Then to begin, they say you sleep too much,
By which they judge your Majesty too sensual,
Apt to decline your strength to ease and pleasures,

And when you do not sleep, you drink too much,
From which they fear suspicions first, then ruines;
And when ye neither drink nor sleep, ye wench much,
Which they affirm first breaks your understanding,
Then takes the edge of Honour, makes us seem,
That are the ribs, and rampires of the Empire,
Fencers, and beaten Fools, and so regarded;
But I believe 'em not; for were these truths,
Your vertue can correct them.

EMPEROUR
They speak plainly.

ÆCIUS
They say moreover (since your Grace will have it,
For they will talk their freedoms, though the Sword
Were in their throat) that of late time, like Nero,
And with the same forgetfulness of glory,
You have got a vein of fidling, so they term it.

EMPEROUR
Some drunken dreams, Æcius.

ÆCIUS
So I hope, Sir:
And that you rather study cruelty,
And to be fear'd for blood, than lov'd for bounty,
Which makes the Nations, as they say, despise ye,
Telling your years and actions by their deaths,
Whose truth and strength of duty made you Cæsar:
They say besides you nourish strange devourers,
Fed with the fat o'th' Empire, they call Bawds,
Lazie and lustful Creatures that abuse ye,
A People as they term 'em, made of paper,
In which the secret sins of each man's monies
Are seal'd and sent a working.

EMPEROUR
What sin's next?
For I perceive they have no mind to spare me.

ÆCIUS
Nor hurt you o' my soul, Sir; but such People
(Nor can the power of man restrain it)
When they are full of meat and ease, must prattle.

EMPEROUR
Forward.

ÆCIUS
I have spoken too much, Sir.

EMPEROUR
I'll have all.

ÆCIUS
It fits not
Your ears should hear their Vanities; no profit
Can justly rise to you from their behaviour,
Unless ye were guilty of those crimes.

EMPEROUR
It may be
I am so, therefore forward.

ÆCIUS
I have ever
Learn'd to obey, nor shall my life resist it.

EMPEROUR
No more Apologies.

ÆCIUS
They grieve besides, Sir,
To see the Nations, whom our ancient Vertue
With many a weary march and hunger conquer'd,
With loss of many a daring life subdu'd,
Fall from their fair obedience, and even murmur
To see the warlike Eagles mew their honours
In obscure Towns, that wont to prey on Princes,
They cry for Enemies, and tell the Captains
The fruits of Italy are luscious, give us Egypt,
Or sandy Africk to display our valours,
There where our Swords may make us meat, and danger
Digest our well got Vyands; here our weapons
And bodies that were made for shining brass,
Are both unedg'd and old with ease and women.
And then they cry again, where are the Germans,
Lin'd with hot Spain, or Gallia, bring 'em on,
And let the Son of War, steel'd Mithridates,
Lead up his winged Parthians like a storm,
Hiding the face of Heaven with showrs of Arrows?
Yet we dare fight like Romans; then as Souldiers
Tir'd with a weary march, they tell their wounds
Even weeping ripe they were no more nor deeper,
And glory in those scars that make them lovely,

And sitting where a Camp was, like sad Pilgrims
They reckon up the times, and living labours
Of Julius or Germanicus, and wonder
That Rome, whose Turrets once were topt with Honours,
Can now forget the Custom of her Conquests;
And then they blame your Grace, and say Who leads us,
Shall we stand here like Statues? were our Fathers
The Sons of lazie Moors, our Princes Persians,
Nothing but silks and softness? Curses on 'em
That first taught Nero wantonness and blood,
Tiberius doubts, Caligula all vices;
For from the spring of these, succeeding Princes—
Thus they talk, Sir.

EMPEROUR
Well,
Why do you hear these things?

ÆCIUS
Why do you do 'em?
I take the gods to witness, with more sorrow,
And more vexation do I hear these tainters
Than were my life dropt from me through an hour-glass.

EMPEROUR
Belike then you believe 'em, or at least
Are glad they should be so; take heed, you were better
Build your own Tomb, and run into it living,
Than dare a Princes anger.

ÆCIUS
I am old, Sir,
And ten years more addition, is but nothing;
Now if my life be pleasing to ye, take it,
Upon my knees, if ever any service,
(As let me brag some have been worthy notice)
If ever any worth, or trust ye gave me
Deserv'd a fair respect, if all my actions,
The hazards of my youth, colds, burnings, wants,
For you, and for the Empire, be not vices;
By that stile ye have stampt upon me, Souldier,
Let me not fall into the hands of Wretches.

EMPEROUR
I understand you not.

ÆCIUS
Let not this body

That has look'd bravely in his blood for Cæsar,
And covetous of wounds, and for your safety,
After the 'scape of Swords, Spears, Slings, and Arrows,
'Gainst which my beaten body was mine armour,
The Seas and thirsty Desarts now be purchase
For Slaves, and base Informers; I see anger,
And death look through your Eyes; I am markt for slaughter,
And know the telling of this truth has made me
A man clean lost to this World; I embrace it;
Only my last Petition, sacred Cæsar,
Is, I may dye a Roman.

EMPEROUR
Rise, my friend still,
And worthy of my love, reclaim the Souldier,
I'll study to do so upon my self too,
Go, keep your Command, and prosper.

ÆCIUS
Life to Cæsar—

[Exit **ÆCIUS**.

[Enter **CHILAX**.

CHILAX
Lord Maximus attends your Grace.

EMPEROUR
Go tell him
I'll meet him in the Gallery:
The honesty of this Æcius,
Who is indeed the Bull-wark of the Empire,
Has div'd so deep into me, that of all
The sins I covet, but this Womans beauty,
With much repentance now I could be quit of;
But she is such a pleasure, being good,
That though I were a god, she'd fire my blood.

[Exeunt.

ACTUS SECUNDUS

SCÆNA PRIMA

Enter the **EMPEROUR, MAXIMUS, LICINIUS, PROCOLUS, CHILAX**, as at Dice.

EMPEROUR
Nay ye shall set my hand out, 'tis not just
I should neglect my fortune now 'tis prosperous.

LICINIUS
If I have any thing to set your Grace,
But Cloaths or good conditions, let me perish.
You have all my money, Sir.

PROCULUS
And mine.

CHILAX
And mine too.

MAXIMUS
Unless your Grace will credit us.

EMPEROUR
No bare board.

LICINIUS
Then at my Garden-House.

EMPEROUR
The Orchard too.

LICINIUS
And't please your Grace.

EMPEROUR
Have at 'em.

PROCULUS
They are lost.

LICINIUS
Why, farewel Fig-trees.

EMPEROUR
Who sets more?

CHILAX
At my horse, Sir.

EMPEROUR
The dapl'd Spaniard?

CHILAX
He.

EMPEROUR
He's mine.

CHILAX
He is so.

MAXIMUS
Your short horse is soon curried.

CHILAX
So it seems, Sir,
So may your Mare be too, if luck serve.

MAXIMUS
Ha?

CHILAX
Nothing my Lord, but grieving at my fortune.

EMPEROUR
Come Maximus, you were not wont to flinch thus.

MAXIMUS
I have lost all.

EMPEROUR
There's a Ring yet.

MAXIMUS
This was not made to lose, Sir.

EMPEROUR
Some love token;
Set it I say.

MAXIMUS
I do beseech your Grace,
Rather name any house I have.

EMPEROUR
How strange
And curious you are grown of toys! redeem't
If so I win it, when you please, to morrow,
Or next day, as you will, I care not,

But only for my lucks sake; 'tis not Rings
Can make me richer.

MAXIMUS
Will you throw, Sir? there 'tis.

EMPEROUR
Why, then have at it fairly, mine.

MAXIMUS
Your Grace
Is only ever fortunate; to morrow,
And't be your pleasure, Sir, I'll pay the price on't.

EMPEROUR
To morrow you shall have it without price, Sir,
But this day 'tis my Victory; good Maximus,
Now I bethink my self, go to Æcius,
And bid him muster all the Cohorts presently;
They mutiny for pay I hear, and be you
Assistant to him; when you know their numbers,
Ye shall have monies for 'em, and above,
Something to stop their tongues withal.

MAXIMUS
I will Sir,
And gods preserve you in this mind still.

EMPEROUR
Shortly I'll see 'em march my self.

MAXIMUS
Gods ever keep ye—

[Exit **MAXIMUS**.

EMPEROUR
To what end do you think this Ring shall serve now?
For ye are Fellows only know by rote,
As Birds record their lessons.

CHILAX
For the Lady.

EMPEROUR
But how for her?

CHILAX

That I confess I know not.

EMPEROUR
Then pray for him that does: fetch me an Eunuch
That never saw her yet; and you two see
The Court made like a Paradise.

[Exit **CHILAX**.

LICINIUS
We will, Sir.

EMPEROUR
Full of fair shews and Musicks; all your arts
(As I shall give instructions) screw to th' highest,
For my main piece is now a doing; and for fear
You should not take, I'll have another Engine,
Such as if vertue be not only in her,
She shall not chuse but lean to, let the Women
Put on a graver shew of welcome.

PROCULUS
Well Sir.

EMPEROUR
They are a thought too eager.

[Enter **CHILAX** and **LYCIAS the EUNUCH**.

CHILAX
Here's the Eunuch.

LYCIAS
Long life to Cæsar.

EMPEROUR
I must use you, Lycias:
Come, let's walk in, and then I'll shew ye all,
If women may be frail, this wench shall fall.

[Exeunt.

SCÆNA SECUNDA

Enter **CLAUDIA** and **MARCELLINA**.

CLAUDIA
Sirrah, what ails my Lady that of late
She never cares for Company?

MARCELLINA
I know not,
Unless it be that Company causes Cuckolds.

CLAUDIA
That were a childish fear.

MARCELLINA
What were those Ladies,
Came to her lately
From the Court?

CLAUDIA
The same wench,
Some grave instructors on my life, they look
For all the world like old hatcht hilts.

MARCELLINA
'Tis true, Wench,
For here and there, and yet they painted well too,
One might discover where the Gold was worn,
Their iron ages.

CLAUDIA
If my judgement fail not,
They have been sheathed like rotten Ships.

MARCELLINA
It may be.

CLAUDIA
For if you mark their rudders, they hang weakly.

MARCELLINA
They have past the line belike; wouldst live Claudia
Till thou wert such as they are?

CLAUDIA
Chimney pieces:
Now heaven have mercy upon me, and young men,
I had rather make a drallery till thirty,
While I am able to endure a tempest,
And bear my fights out bravely, till my tackle
Whistl'd i'th' Wind, and held against all weathers,

While I were able to bear with my tyres,
And so discharge 'em, I would willingly
Live, Marcellina, not till barnacles
Bred in my sides.

MARCELLINA
Thou art i'th' right, Wench;
For who would live whom pleasures had forsaken,
To stand at mark, and cry a Bow short, Seigneur?
Were there not men came hither too?

CLAUDIA
Brave fellows:
I fear me Bawds of five i'th' Pound.

MARCELLINA
How know you?

CLAUDIA
They gave me great lights to it.

MARCELLINA
Take heed, Claudia.

CLAUDIA
Let them take heed, the spring comes on.

MARCELLINA
To me now
They seem'd as noble Visitants.

CLAUDIA
To me now
Nothing less, Marcellina, for I markt 'em,
And by this honest light, for yet 'tis morning,
Saving the reverence of their gilded doublets,
And Millan skins.

MARCELLINA
Thou art a strange Wench, Claudia.

CLAUDIA
Ye are deceiv'd, they shew'd to me directly
Court Crabs that creep a side-way for their living,
I know 'em by the Breeches that they beg'd last.

MARCELLINA
Peace, my Lady comes; what may that be?

[Enter **LUCINA** and **LYCIAS the EUNUCH**.

CLAUDIA
A Sumner
That cites her to appear.

MARCELLINA
No more of that wench.

LYCIAS
Madam, what answer to your Lord?

LUCINA
Pray tell him, I am subject to his will.

LYCIAS
Why weep you Madam?
Excellent Lady, there are none will hurt you.

LUCINA
I do beseech you tell me Sir.

LYCIAS
What, Lady?

LUCINA
Serve ye the Emperor?

LYCIAS
I do.

LUCINA
In what place?

LYCIAS
In's chamber Madam.

LUCINA
Do ye serve his will too?

LYCIAS
In fair and just commands.

LUCINA
Are ye a Roman?

LYCIAS

Yes noble Lady, and a Mantuan.

LUCINA
What office bore your parents?

LYCIAS
One was Pretor.

LUCINA
Take heed then how you stain his reputation.

LYCIAS
Why worthy Lady?

LUCINA
If ye know, I charge ye,
Ought in this Message, but what honesty,
The trust and fair obedience of a servant
May well deliver, yet take heed, and help me.

LYCIAS
Madam, I am no Broker.

CLAUDIA
I'le be hang'd then.

LYCIAS
Nor base procurer of mens lusts; Your husband,
Pray'd me to do this office, I have done it,
It rests in you to come, or no.

LUCINA
I will Sir.

LYCIAS
If ye mistrust me, do not.

LUCINA
Ye appear so worthy,
And to all my sense so honest,
And this is such a certain sign ye have brought me,
That I believe.

LYCIAS
Why should I cozen you?
Or were I brib'd to do this villany,
Can mony prosper, or the fool that takes it,
When such a vertue falls?

LUCINA
Ye speak well Sir;
Would all the rest that serve the Emperour,
Had but your way.

CLAUDIA
And so they have ad unguem.

LUCINA
Pray tell my Lord, I have receiv'd his Token,
And will not fail to meet him; yet good Sir, thus much
Before you goe, I do beseech ye too,
As little notice as ye can, deliver
Of my appearance there.

LYCIAS
It shall be Madam,
And so I wish you happiness.

LUCINA
I thank you—

[Exeunt.

SCÆNA TERTIA

Tumult & noise within.

Enter **ÆCIUS**, pursuing **PONTIUS**, the Captain and **MAXIMUS**, following.

MAXIMUS
Temper your self Æcius.

PONTIUS
Hold my Lord,
I am a Roman, and a Souldier.

MAXIMUS
Pray Sir.

ÆCIUS
Thou art a lying Villain, and a Traytor;
Give me my self, or by the Gods my friend
You'l make me dangerous; how dar'st thou pluck
The Souldiers to sedition, and I living,

And sow Rebellion in 'em, and even then
When I am drawing out to action?

PONTIUS
Hear me.

MAXIMUS
Are ye a man?

ÆCIUS
I am a true hearted, Maximus,
And if the Villain live, we are dishonour'd.

MAXIMUS
But hear him what he can say.

ÆCIUS
That's the way,
To pardon him; I am so easie natur'd,
That if he speak but humbly I forgive him.

PONTIUS
I do beseech ye noble General.

ÆCIUS
Has found the way already, give me room,
One stroak, and if he scape me then h'as mercy.

PONTIUS
I do not call ye noble, that I fear ye,
I never car'd for death; if ye will kill me,
Consider first for what, not what you can do;
'Tis true, I know ye for my General,
And by that great Prerogative may kill:
But do it justly then.

ÆCIUS
He argues with me,
A made up Rebel.

MAXIMUS
Pray consider,
What certain grounds ye have for this.

ÆCIUS
What grounds?
Did I not take him preaching to the Souldiers
How lazily they liv'd, and what dishonours

It was to serve a Prince so full of woman?
Those were his very words, friend.

MAXIMUS
These, Æcius,
Though they were rashly spoke, which was an errour
(A great one Pontius) yet from him that hungers
For wars, and brave imployment, might be pardon'd.
The heart, and harbour'd thoughts of ill, make Traytors,
Not spleeny speeches.

ÆCIUS
Why should you protect him?
Goe to, it shews not honest.

MAXIMUS
Taint me not,
For that shews worse Æcius: All your friendship
And that pretended love ye lay upon me,
Hold back my honesty, is like a favour
You do your slave to day, to morrow hang him,
Was I your bosome piece for this?

ÆCIUS
Forgive me,
The nature of my zeal, and for my Country,
Makes me sometimes forget my self; for know,
Though I most strive to be without my passions,
I am no God: For you Sir, whose infection
Has spread it self like poyson through the army,
And cast a killing fog on fair allegiance,
First thank this noble Gentleman, ye had dy'd else;
Next from your place, and honour of a Souldier,
I here seclude you.

PONTIUS
May I speak yet?

MAXIMUS
Hear him.

ÆCIUS
And while Aecius holds a reputation,
At least command, ye bear no arms for Rome Sir.

PONTIUS
Against her I shall never: the condemn'd man
Has yet that priviledge to speak, my Lord;

Law were not equall else.

MAXIMUS
Pray hear Aecius,
For happily the fault he has committed,
Though I believe it mighty, yet considered,
If mercy may be thought upon, will prove
Rather a hastie sin, than heynous.

ÆCIUS
Speak.

PONTIUS
'Tis true my Lord, ye took me tir'd with peace,
My words almost as ragged as my fortunes.
'Tis true I told the Souldier, whom we serv'd,
And then bewail'd, we had an Emperour
Led from us by the flourishes of Fencers;
I blam'd him too for women.

ÆCIUS
To the rest Sir.

PONTIUS
And like enough I blest him then as Souldiers
Will do sometimes: 'Tis true I told 'em too,
We lay at home, to show our Country
We durst goe naked, durst want meat, and mony,
And when the slave drinks wine, we durst be thirstie:
I told 'em this too, that the Trees and Roots
Were our best pay-masters; the Charity
Of longing women, that had bought our bodies,
Our beds, fires, Taylers, Nurses. Nay I told 'em,
(For you shall hear the greatest sin, I said Sir)
By that time there be wars again, our bodies
Laden with scarrs, and aches, and ill lodgings,
Heats, and perpetual wants, were fitter prayers
And certain graves, than cope the foe on crutches:
'Tis likely too, I counsell'd 'em to turn
Their warlike pikes to plough-shares, their sure Targets
And Swords hatcht with the bloud of many Nations,
To Spades, and pruning Knives, for those get mony,
Their warlike Eagles, into Daws, or Starlings,
To give an Ave Cæsar as he passes,
And be rewarded with a thousand drachma's,
For thus we get but years and beets.

ÆCIUS

What think you,
Were these words to be spoken by a Captain,
One that should give example?

MAXIMUS
'Twas too much.

PONTIUS
My Lord, I did not wooe 'em from the Empire,
Nor bid 'em turn their daring steel 'gainst Cæsar,
The Gods for ever hate me, if that motion
Were part of me: Give me but imployment, Sir;
And way to live, and where you hold me vicious,
Bred up in mutiny, my Sword shall tell ye,
And if you please, that place I held, maintain it,
'Gainst the most daring foes of Rome. I am honest,
A lover of my Country, one that holds
His life no longer his, than kept for Cæsar.
Weigh not (I thus low on my knee beseech you)
What my rude tongue discovered, 'twas my want,
No other part of Pontius: you have seen me,
And you my Lord, do something for my Country,
And both beheld the wounds I gave and took,
Not like a backward Traytor.

ÆCIUS
All this language
Makes but against you Pontius, you are cast,
And by mine honour, and my love to Cæsar,
By me shall never be restor'd; In my Camp
I will not have a tongue, though to himself
Dare talk but near sedition; as I govern,
All shall obey, and when they want, their duty
And ready service shall redress their needs,
Not prating what they would be.

PONTIUS
Thus I leave ye,
Yet shall my prayers still, although my fortunes
Must follow you no more, be still about ye,
Gods give ye where ye fight the Victory,
Ye cannot cast my wishes.

ÆCIUS
Come my Lord,
Now to the Field again.

MAXIMUS

Alas poor Pontius.—

[Exeunt.

Enter **CHILAX**, at one door, **LICINIUS**, and **BALBUS**, at another.

LICINIUS
How how?

CHILAX
She's come.

BALBUS
Then I'le to th' Emperour.—

[Exit **BALBUS**.

CHILAX
Do; Is the Musick placed well?

LICINIUS
Excellent.

CHILAX
Licinius, you and Proclus receive her
In the great Chamber, at her entrance,
Let me alone; and do you hear Licinius,
Pray let the Ladies ply her further off,
And with much more discretion: one word more.

LICINIUS
Well.

CHILAX
Are the Jewels, and those ropes of Pearl,

[Enter **EMPEROUR**, **BALBUS** and **PROCULUS**.

Laid in the way she passes?

LICINIUS
Take no care man—

[Exit **LICINIUS**.

EMPEROUR
What is she come?

CHILAX
She is Sir; but 'twere best,
Your Grace were seen last to her.

EMPEROUR
So I mean;
Keep the Court emptie Proculus.

PROCULUS
'Tis done Sir.

EMPEROUR
Be not too sudden to her.

CHILAX
Good your Grace,
Retire, and man your self; let us alone,
We are no children this way: do you hear Sir?
'Tis necessary that her waiting women
Be cut off in the Lobby, by some Ladies,
They'd break the business else.

EMPEROUR
'Tis true, they shall.

CHILAX
Remember your place Proculus.

PROCULUS
I warrant ye.—

[Exeunt **EMPEROUR, BALBUS** and **PROCULUS.**

[Enter **LUCINA, CLAUDIA** and **MARCELLINA.**

CHILAX
She enters: who are waiters there? the Emperour
Calls for his Horse to air himself.

LUCINA
I am glad,
I come so happily to take him absent,
This takes away a little fear; I know him,
Now I begin to fear again: O honour,

If ever thou hadst temple in weak woman,
And sacrifice of modesty burnt to thee,
Hold me fast now, and help me.

CHILAX
Noble Madam,
Ye are welcom to the Court, most nobly welcom,
Ye are a stranger Lady.

LUCINA
I desire so.

CHILAX
A wondrous stranger here,
Nothing so strange:
And therefore need a guide I think.

LUCINA
I do Sir,
And that a good one too.

CHILAX
My service Lady,
Shall be your guide in this place; But pray ye tell me,
Are ye resolv'd a Courtier?

LUCINA
No I hope Sir.

CLAUDIA
You are, Sir?

CHILAX
Yes, my fair one.

CLAUDIA
So it seems,
You are so ready to bestow your self,
Pray what might cost those Breeches?

CHILAX
Would you wear 'em?
Madam ye have a witty woman.

MARCELLINA
Two Sir,
Or else ye underbuy us.

LUCINA
Leave your talking:
But is my Lord here, I beseech ye, Sir?

CHILAX
He is sweet Lady, and must take this kindly,
Exceeding kindly of ye, wondrous kindly
Ye come so far to visit him: I'le guide ye.

LUCINA
Whither?

CHILAX
Why to your Lord.

LUCINA
Is it so hard Sir,
To find him in this place without a Guide?
For I would willingly not trouble you.

CHILAX
It will be so for you that are a stranger;
Nor can it be a trouble to do service
To such a worthy beauty, and besides—

MARCELLINA
I see he will goe with us.

CLAUDIA
Let him amble.

CHILAX
It fits not that a Lady of your reckoning
Should pass without attendants.

LUCINA
I have two Sir.

CHILAX
I mean without a man; You'l see the Emperour?

LUCINA
Alas I am not fit Sir.

CHILAX
You are well enough,
He'l take it wondrous kindly: Hark.

LUCINA
Ye flatter,
Good Sir, no more of that.

CHILAX
Well, I but tell ye.

LUCINA
Will ye goe forward, since I must be man'd,
Pray take your place.

CLAUDIA
Cannot ye man us too Sir?

CHILAX
Give me but time.

MARCELLINA
And you'l try all things.

CHILAX
No:
I'le make no such promise.

CLAUDIA
If ye do Sir,
Take heed ye stand to't.

CHILAX
Wondrous merry Ladies.

[Exit.

[Enter **LICINIUS** and **PROCULUS, BALBUS**.

LUCINA
The wenches are dispos'd, pray keep your way Sir.

LICINIUS
She is coming up the stairs; Now the Musick;
And as that stirs her, let's set on: perfumes there.

PROCULUS
Discover all the Jewels.

LICINIUS
Peace.

[Musick.

Now the lusty Spring is seen,
Golden yellow, gaudy Blew,
Daintily invite the view.
Every where, on every Green,
Roses blushing as they blow,
And inticing men to pull,
Lillies whiter than the snow,
Woodbines of sweet hony full.
All Loves Emblems and all cry,
Ladys, if not pluckt we dye.

Yet the lusty Spring hath staid,
Blushing red and purest white,
Daintily to love invite,
Every Woman, every Maid,
Cherries kissing as they grow;
And inviting men to taste,
Apples even ripe below,
Winding gently to the waste:
All loves emblems and all cry,
Ladies, if not pluckt we dye.

[**SECOND**.
Hear ye Ladies that despise
What the mighty Love has done,
Fear examples, and be wise,
Fair Calisto was a Nun,
Læda sailing on the stream,
To deceive the hopes of man,
Love accounting but a dream,
Doted on a silver Swan,
Danae in a Brazen Tower,
Where no love was, lov'd a Showr.

Hear ye Ladys that are coy,
What the mighty Love can do,
Fear the fierceness of the Boy,
The chaste Moon he makes to wooe:
Vesta kindling holy fires,
Circled round about with spies,
Never dreaming loose desires,
Doting at the Altar dies.
Ilion in a short hour higher
He can build, and once more fire.

[Enter **CHILAX**, **LUCINA**, **CLAUDIA** and **MARCELLINA**.

LUCINA
Pray Heaven my Lord be here, for now I fear it.
Well Ring, if thou bee'st counterfeit, or stoln,
As by this preparation I suspect it,
Thou hast betrai'd thy Mistris: pray Sir forward,
I would fain see my Lord.

CHILAX
But tell me Madam,
How do ye like the Song?

LUCINA
I like the air well,
But for the words, they are lascivious,
And over light for Ladies.

CHILAX
All ours love 'em.

LUCINA
'Tis like enough, for yours are loving Ladies.

LICINIUS
Madam, ye are welcom to the Court. Who waits?
Attendants for this Lady.

LUCINA
Ye mistake Sir;
I bring no triumph with me.

LICINIUS
But much honour.

PROCULUS
Why this was nobly done; and like a neighbour,
So freely of your self to be a visitant,
The Emperour shall give ye thanks for this.

LUCINA
O no Sir;
There's nothing to deserve 'em.

PROCULUS
Yes, your presence.

LUCINA

Good Gentlemen be patient, and believe
I come to see my husband, on command too,
I were no Courtier else.

LICINIUS
That's all one Lady,
Now ye are here, y'are welcom, and the Emperour
Who loves ye, but too well.

LUCINA
No more of that Sir.
I came not to be Catechiz'd.

PROCULUS
Ah Sirrah;
And have we got you here? faith Noble Lady,
We'l keep you one month Courtier.

LUCINA
Gods defend Sir,
I never lik'd a trade worse.

PROCULUS
Hark ye.

LUCINA
No Sir.

PROCULUS
Ye are grown the strangest Lady.

LUCINA
How?

PROCULUS
By Heaven,
'Tis true I tell ye, and you'l find it.

LUCINA
I?
I'le rather find my grave, and so inform him.

PROCULUS
Is it not pity Gentlemen, this Lady,
(Nay I'le deal roughly with ye, yet not hurt ye)
Should live alone, and give such heavenly beauty
Only to walls, and hangings?

LUCINA
Good Sir, patience:
I am no wonder, neither come to that end,
Ye do my Lord an injury to stay me,
Who though ye are the Princes, yet dare tell ye
He keeps no wife for your wayes.

BALBUS
Well, well Lady;
However you are pleas'd to think of us,
Ye are welcom, and ye shall be welcome.

LUCINA
Shew it
In that I come for then, in leading me
Where my lov'd Lord is, not in flattery:—

[Jewels shew'd.

Nay ye may draw the Curtain, I have seen 'em,
But none worth half my honesty.

CLAUDIA
Are these Sir,
Laid here to take?

PROCULUS
Yes, for your Lady, Gentlewomen.

MARCELLINA
We had been doing else.

BALBUS
Meaner Jewels
Would fit your worths.

CLAUDIA
And meaner clothes your bodies.

LUCINA
The Gods shall kill me first.

LICINIUS
There's better dying;
I'th' Emperours arms goe to, but be not angry—
These are but talks sweet Lady.

[Enter **PHORBA** and **ARDELIA**.

PHORBA
Where is this stranger? rushes, Ladys, rushes,
Rushes as green as Summer for this stranger.

PROCULUS
Here's Ladies come to see you.

LUCINA
You are gone then?
I take it 'tis your Qu.

PROCULUS
Or rather manners,
You are better fitted Madam, we but tire ye,
Therefore we'l leave you for an hour, and bring
Your much lov'd Lord unto you—

[Exeunt.

LUCINA
Then I'le thank ye,
I am betrai'd for certain; well Lucina,
If thou do'st fall from vertue, may the Earth
That after death should shoot up gardens of thee,
Spreading thy living goodness into branches,
Fly from thee, and the hot Sun find thy vices.

PHORBA
You are a welcom woman.

ARDELIA
Bless me Heaven,
How did you find the way to Court?

LUCINA
I know not,
Would I had never trod it.

PHORBA
Prethee tell me,
Good noble Lady, and good sweet heart love us,
For we love thee extreamly; is not this place
A Paradise to live in?

LUCINA
To those people
That know no other Paradise but pleasure,

That little I enjoy contents me better.

ARDELIA
What, heard ye any Musick yet?

LUCINA
Too much.

PHORBA
You must not be thus froward; what, this gown
Is one o'th' prettiest by my troth Ardelia,
I ever saw yet; 'twas not to frown in Lady,
Ye put this gown on when ye came.

ARDELIA
How do ye?
Alas poor wretch how cold it is!

LUCINA
Content ye;
I am as well as may be, and as temperate,
If ye will let me be so: where's my Lord?
For there's the business that I came for Ladies.

PHORBA
We'l lead ye to him, he's i'th' Gallery.

ARDELIA
We'l shew ye all the Court too.

LUCINA
Shew me him,
And ye have shew'd me all I come to look on.

PHORBA
Come on, we'l be your guides, and as ye goe,
We have some pretty tales to tell ye Lady,
Shall make ye merry too; ye come not here,
To be a sad Lucina.

LUCINA
Would I might not.—

[Exeunt.

[Enter **CHILAX** and **BALBUS**.

CHILAX

Now the soft Musick; Balbus run—

BALBUS
I flye Boy—

[Exit **BALBUS**.

CHILAX
The women by this time are worming of her,—
If she can hold out them, the Emperour

[Musick.

Takes her to task: he has her; hark the Musick.

[Enter **EMPEROUR** and **LUCINA**.

LUCINA
Good your Grace,
Where are my women Sir?

EMPEROUR
They are wise, beholding
What you think scorn to look on, the Courts bravery:
Would you have run away so slily Lady,
And not have seen me?

LUCINA
I beseech your Majestie,
Consider what I am, and whose.

EMPEROUR
I do so.

LUCINA
Believe me, I shall never make a whore Sir.

EMPEROUR
A friend ye may, and to that man that loves ye,
More than you love your vertue.

LUCINA
Sacred Cæsar.

EMPEROUR
You shall not kneel to me sweet.

LUCINA

Look upon me,
And if ye be so cruel to abuse me,
Think how the Gods will take it; does this beauty
Afflict your soul? I'le hide it from you ever,
Nay more, I will become so leprous,
That ye shall curse me from ye: My dear Lord
Has serv'd ye ever truly, fought your Battels,
As if he daily long'd to dye for Cæsar,
Was never Traytor Sir, nor never tainted
In all the actions of his life.

EMPEROUR
I know it.

LUCINA
His fame and family have grown together,
And spred together like to sailing Cedars,
Over the Roman Diadem; O let not,
As ye have any flesh that's humane in you,
The having of a modest wife decline him,
Let not my vertue be the wedge to break him.
I do not think ye are lascivious,
These wanton men belye ye, you are Cæsar,
Which is the Father of the Empires honour,
Ye are too near the nature of the Gods,
To wrong the weakest of all creatures, women.

EMPEROUR
I dare not do it here, rise fair Lucina,
I did but try your temper, ye are honest,
And with the commendations wait on that
I'le lead ye to your Lord, and give you to him:
Wipe your fair eyes: he that endeavours ill,
May well delay, but never quench his hell.—

[Exeunt.

ACTUS TERTIUS

SCÆNA PRIMA

Enter **CHILAX, LICINIUS, PROCULUS** and **BALBUS**.

CHILAX
'Tis done Licinius.

LICINIUS
How?

CHILAX
I shame to tell it,
If there be any justice, we are Villains,
And must be so rewarded.

BALBUS
If it be done,
I take it 'tis no time now to repent it,
Let's make the best o'th' trade.

PROCULUS
Now vengeance take it,
Why should not he have setled on a beauty,
Whose honesty stuck in a piece of tissue,
Or one a Ring might rule, or such a one
That had an itching husband to be honourable,
And ground to get it: if he must have women,
And no allay without 'em, why not those
That know the misery, and are best able
To play a game with judgement? such as she is,
Grant they be won with long siege, endless travel,
And brought to opportunity with millions,
Yet when they come to motion, their cold vertue
Keeps 'em like cakes of Ice; I'le melt a Crystal,
And make a dead flint fire himself, e're they
Give greater heat, than new departing embers
Give to old men that watch 'em.

LICINIUS
A good Whore
Had sav'd all this, and happily as wholsom,
I, and the thing once done too, as well thought of,
But this same chastity forsooth.

PROCULUS
A Pox on't,
Why should not women be as free as we are?
They are, but not in open, and far freer,
And the more bold ye bear your self, more welcom,
And there is nothing you dare say, but truth,
But they dare hear.—

[Enter **EMPEROUR** and **LUCINA**.

CHILAX

The Emperour! away,
And if we can repent, let's home and pray.

[Exeunt.

EMPEROUR
Your only vertue now is patience,
Take heed, and save your honour; if you talk.

LUCINA
As long as there is motion in my body,
And life to give me words, I'le cry for justice.

EMPEROUR
Justice shall never hear ye, I am justice.

LUCINA
Wilt thou not kill me, Monster, Ravisher,
Thou bitter bane o'th' Empire, look upon me,
And if thy guilty eyes dare see these ruines,
Thy wild lust hath laid level with dishonour,
The sacrilegious razing of this Temple,
The mother of thy black sins would have blush'd at,
Behold and curse thy self; the Gods will find thee,
That's all my refuge now, for they are righteous,
Vengeance and horror circle thee; the Empire,
In which thou liv'st a strong continued surfeit,
Like poyson will disgorge thee, good men raze thee
For ever being read again,—but vicious
Women, and fearfull Maids, make vows against thee:
Thy own Slaves, if they hear of this, shall hate thee;
And those thou hast corrupted first fall from thee;
And if thou let'st me live, the Souldier,
Tir'd with thy Tyrannies, break through obedience,
And shake his strong Steel at thee.

EMPEROUR
This prevails not;
Nor any Agony ye utter Lady,
If I have done a sin, curse her that drew me,
Curse the first cause, the witchcraft that abus'd me,
Curse those fair eyes, and curse that heavenly beauty,
And curse your being good too.

LUCINA
Glorious thief,
What restitution canst thou make to save me?

EMPEROUR
I'le ever love, and honour you.

LUCINA
Thou canst not,
For that which was mine honour, thou hast murdred,
And can there be a love in violence?

EMPEROUR
You shall be only mine.

LUCINA
Yet I like better
Thy villany, than flattery, that's thine own,
The other basely counterfeit; flye from me,
Or for thy safety sake and wisdom kill me,
For I am worse than thou art; thou maist pray,
And so recover grace; I am lost for ever,
And if thou let'st me live, th'art lost thy self too.

EMPEROUR
I fear no loss but love, I stand above it.

LUCINA
Call in your Lady Bawds, and guilded Pander's
And let them triumph too, and sing to Cæsar,
Lucina's faln, the chast Lucina's conquer'd;
Gods! what a wretched thing has this man made me!
For I am now no wife for Maximus,
No company for women that are vertuous,
No familie I now can claim, nor Country,
Nor name, but Cæsar's whore; O sacred Cæsar,
(For that should be your title) was your Empire,
Your Rods, and Axes, that are types of Justice,
Those fires that ever burn, to beg you blessings,
The peoples adoration, fear of Nations,
What victory can bring ye home, what else
The usefull Elements can make your servants,
Even light it self, and suns of light, truth, Justice,
Mercy, and starlike pietie sent to you,
And from the gods themselves, to ravish women?
The curses that I owe to Enemies,
Even those the Sabines sent, when Romulus,
(As thou hast me) ravish'd their noble Maids,
Made more, and heavier, light on thee.

EMPEROUR
This helps not.

LUCINA

The sins of Tarquin be remember'd in thee,
And where there has a chast wife been abus'd,
Let it be thine, the shame thine, thine the slaughter,
And last for ever thine, the fear'd example.
Where shall poor vertue live, now I am faln?
What can your honours now, and Empire make me,
But a more glorious Whore?

EMPEROUR

A better woman,
But if ye will be blind, and scorn it, who can help it?
Come leave these lamentations, they do nothing,
But make a noyse, I am the same man still,
Were it to do again; therefore be wiser,
By all this holy light, I should attempt it,
Ye are so excellent, and made to ravish,
There were no pleasure in ye else.

LUCINA

Oh villain.

EMPEROUR

So bred for mans amazement, that my reason
And every help to hold me right has lost me;
The God of love himself had been before me
Had he but power to see ye; tell me justly,
How can I choose but err then? if ye dare
Be mine, and only mine, for ye are so pretious,
I envie any other should enjoy ye,
Almost look on ye; and your daring husband
Shall know h'as kept an offring from the Empire,
Too holy for his Altars; be the mightiest,
More than my self I'le make it: if ye will not
Sit down with this, and silence, for which wisdom
Ye shall have use of me, and much honour ever,
And be the same you were; if ye divulge it,
Know I am far above the faults I do,
And those I do I am able to forgive too;
And where your credit in the knowledge of it,
May be with gloss enough suspected, mine
Is as mine own command shall make it:
Princes though they be sometime subject to loose whispers,
Yet wear they two edged swords for open censures:
Your husband cannot help ye, nor the Souldier;
Your husband is my creature, they my weapons,
And only where I bid 'em strike; I feed 'em,

Nor can the Gods be angry at this action,
For as they make me most, they mean me happiest,
Which I had never been without this pleasure:
Consider, and farewell: you'l find your women
At home before ye, they have had some sport too,
But are more thankful for it—

[Exit **EMPEROUR**.

LUCINA
Destruction find thee.
Now which way must I go? my honest house
Will shake to shelter me, my husband flee me,
My Family, because they are honest, and desire to be so,
Must not endure me, not a neighbour know me:
What woman now dare see me without blushes,
And pointing as I pass, there, there, behold her,
Look on her little Children, that is she,
That handsome Lady, mark; O my sad fortunes,
Is this the end of goodness, this the price
Of all my early prayers to protect me,
Why then I see there is no God but power,
Nor vertue now alive that cares for us,
But what is either lame or sensual,
How had I been thus wretched else?

[Enter **MAXIMUS** and **ÆCIUS**.

ÆCIUS
Let Titius
Command the company that Pontius lost,
And see the Fosses deeper.

MAXIMUS
How now sweet heart,
What make you here, and thus?

ÆCIUS
Lucina weeping!
This must be much offence.

MAXIMUS
Look up and tell me,
Why are you thus? My Ring? O friend, I have found it,
Ye are at Court, sweet.

LUCINA
Yes, this brought me hither.

MAXIMUS
Rise, and goe home: I have my fears Aecius:
Oh my best friend, I am ruin'd; go Lucina,
Already in thy tears I have read thy wrongs,
Already found a Cæsar; go thou Lilly,
Thou sweetly drooping flower: go silver Swan,
And sing thine own sad requiem: goe Lucina,
And if thou dar'st, outlive this wrong.

LUCINA
I dare not.

ÆCIUS
Is that the Ring ye lost?

MAXIMUS
That, that, Aecius,
That cursed Ring, my self, and all my fortunes:
'Thas pleas'd the Emperour, my noble master,
For all my services, and dangers for him,
To make me mine own Pander, was this justice?
Oh my Aecius, have I liv'd to bear this?

LUCINA
Farewel for ever Sir.

MAXIMUS
That's a sad saying,
But such a one becomes ye well Lucina:
And yet me thinks we should not part so lightly,
Our loves have been of longer growth, more rooted
Than the sharp word of one farewel can scatter,
Kiss me: I find no Cæsar here; these lips
Taste not of Ravisher in my opinion.
Was it not so?

LUCINA
O yes.

MAXIMUS
I dare believe thee,
For thou wert ever truth it self, and sweetness;
Indeed she was, Æcius.

ÆCIUS
So she is still.

MAXIMUS
Once more, O my Lucina, O my Comfort,
The blessing of my Youth, the life of my life.

ÆCIUS
I have seen enough to stagger my obedience;
Hold me ye equal Gods, this is too sinful.

MAXIMUS
Why wert thou chosen out to make a Whore of?
To me thou wert too chaste; fall Crystal Fountains,
And ever feed your streams you rising sorrows,
Till you have dropt your Mistris into Marble:
Now go for ever from me.

LUCINA
Long farewel, Sir.
And as I have been loyal, gods think on me.

MAXIMUS
Stay, let me once more bid farewel, Lucina,
Farewel thou excellent example of us,
Thou starry Vertue, fare thee well, seek Heaven,
And there by Cassiopea shine in Glory,
We are too base and dirty to preserve thee.

ÆCIUS
Nay, I must kiss too; such a kiss again,
And from a Woman of so ripe a Vertue,
Æcius must not take; Farewel thou Phœnix,
If thou wilt dye, Lucina; which well weigh'd,
If you can cease a while from these strange thoughts,
I wish were rather alter'd.

LUCINA
No.

ÆCIUS
Mistake not;
I would not stain your honour for the Empire,
Nor any way decline you to discredit,
'Tis not my fair profession, but a Villains;
I find and feel your loss as deep as you do,
And am the same, Æcius, still as honest,
The same life I have still for Maximus,
The same Sword wear for you, where Justice wills me,
And 'tis no dull one; therefore misconceive me not;
Only I would have you live a little longer,

But a short year.

MAXIMUS
She must not.

LUCINA
Why so long, Sir,
Am I not grey enough with grief already?

ÆCIUS
To draw from that wild man a sweet repentance,
And goodness in his days to come.

MAXIMUS
They are so,
And will be ever coming, my Æcius.

ÆCIUS
For who knows but the sight of you, presenting
His swoln sins at the full, and your fair vertues,
May like a fearful Vision fright his follies,
And once more bend him right again? which blessing
(If your dark wrongs would give you leave to read)
Is more than death, and the reward more glorious;
Death, only eases you, this, the whole Empire;
Besides, compell'd and forc'd with violence,
To what ye have done, the deed is none of yours,
No, nor the justice neither; ye may live,
And still a worthier Woman, still more honoured;
For are those trees the worse we tear the fruits from?
Or should the eternal gods desire to perish
Because we daily violate their truths,
Which is the Chastity of Heaven? No, Lady,
If ye dare live, ye may; and as our sins
Make them more full of equity and justice,
So this compulsive wrong makes you more perfect;
The Empire too will bless you.

MAXIMUS
Noble Sir,
If she were any thing to me but honour,
And that that's wedded to me too, laid in,
Not to be worn away without my being;
Or could the wrongs be hers alone, or mine,
Or both our wrongs, not ty'd to after issues,
Not born anew in all our names and kindreds,
I would desire her live, nay more, compel her:
But since it was not Youth, but Malice did it,

And not her own, nor mine, but both our losses,
Nor stays it there, but that our names must find it,
Even those to come; and when they read, she liv'd,
Must they not ask how often she was ravish'd,
And make a doubt she lov'd that more than Wedlock?
Therefore she must not live.

ÆCIUS
Therefore she must live,
To teach the world, such deaths are superstitious.

LUCINA
The tongues of Angels cannot alter me,
For could the World again restore my Credit,
As fair and absolute as first I bred it,
That world I should not trust again: The Empire
By my life, can get nothing but my story,
Which whilst I breath must be but his abuses;
And where ye counsel me to live, that Cæsar
May see his errours and repent, I'll tell ye,
His penitence is but encrease of pleasures,
His prayers never said but to deceive us,
And when he weeps (as you think) for his Vices,
'Tis but as killing drops from baleful Yew-Trees,
That rot their honest Neighbour; If he can grieve
As one that yet desires his free Conversion,
And almost glories in his penitence,
I'll leave him Robes to mourn in, my sad ashes.

ÆCIUS
The farewels then of happy souls be with thee,
And to thy memory be ever sung
The praises of a just and constant Lady,
This sad day whilst I live, a Souldiers tears
I'll offer on thy Monument, and bring
Full of thy noble self with tears untold yet,
Many a worthy Wife, to weep thy ruine.

MAXIMUS
All that is chaste upon thy Tomb shall flourish,
All living Epitaphs be thine, Time, Story;
And what is left behind to piece our lives
Shall be no more abus'd with tales and trifles,
But full of thee, stand to eternity.

ÆCIUS
Once more farewel, go find Elyzium,
There where the happy Souls are crown'd with Blessings,

There where 'tis ever Spring and ever Summer.

MAXIMUS
There where no bedrid justice comes; truth, honour,
Are keepers of that blessed Place; go thither,
For here thou liv'st chaste Fire in rotten Timber.

ÆCIUS
And so our last farewels.

MAXIMUS
Gods give thee Justice—

[Exit **LUCINA**.

ÆCIUS
His thoughts begin to work, I fear him, yet
He ever was a noble Roman, but
I know not what to think on't, he hath suffered
Beyond a man if he stand this.

MAXIMUS
Æcius,
Am I alive, or has a dead sleep seiz'd me?
It was my Wife the Emperour abus'd thus,
And I must say I am glad I had her for him;
Must I not, my Æcius?

ÆCIUS
I am stricken
With such a stiff amazement, that no answer
Can readily come from me, nor no comfort;
Will ye go home, or go to my house?

MAXIMUS
Neither;
I have no home, and you are mad, Æcius,
To keep me company, I am a fellow
My own Sword would forsake, not tyed unto me;
A Pander is a Prince, to what I am faln;
I dare do nothing.

ÆCIUS
Ye do better.

MAXIMUS
I am made a branded Slave, Æcius,
And yet I bless the Maker;

Death o' my Soul, must I endure this tamely?
Must Maximus be mention'd for his tales?
I am a Child too; what should I do railing?
I cannot mend my self, 'tis Cæsar did it,
And what am I to him?

ÆCIUS

'Tis well consider'd;
However you are tainted, be no Traitor
Time may outwear the first, the last lives ever.

MAXIMUS

O that thou wert not living, and my friend.

ÆCIUS

I'll bear a wary Eye upon your actions,
I fear ye, Maximus, nor can I blame thee
If thou break'st out, for by the gods thy wrong
Deserves a general ruine: do ye love me?

MAXIMUS

That's all I have to live on.

ÆCIUS

Then go with me,
Ye shall not to your own house.

MAXIMUS

Nor to any.
My griefs are greater far than Walls can compass,
And yet I wonder how it happens with me,
I am not dangerous, and o' my Conscience,
Should I now see the Emperour i'th' heat on't,
I should not chide him for't, an awe runs through me,
I feel it sensibly that binds me to it,
'Tis at my heart now, there it sits and rules,
And methinks 'tis a pleasure to obey it.

ÆCIUS

'This is a mask to cozen me; I know ye,
And how far ye dare do; no Roman farther,
Nor with more fearless Valour; and I'll watch ye,
Keep that obedience still.

MAXIMUS

Is a Wifes loss
(For her abuse much good may do his Grace,
I'll make as bold with his Wife, if I can)

More than the fading of a few fresh colours,
More than a lusty spring lost?

ÆCIUS
No more, Maximus,
To one that truly lives.

MAXIMUS
Why, then I care not, I can live well enough,
For look you friend, for vertue, and those trifles,
They may be bought they say.

ÆCIUS
He's craz'd a little,
His grief has made him talk things from his Nature.

MAXIMUS
But Chastity is not a thing I take it
To get in Rome, unless it be bespoken
A hundred years before; Is it Æcius?
By'r Lady, and well handled too i'th' breeding.

ÆCIUS
Will ye go any way?

MAXIMUS
I'll tell thee, friend;
If my Wife for all this should be a Whore now,
A kind of Kicker out of sheets, 'twould vex me,
For I am not angry yet; the Emperour
Is young and handsome, and the Woman Flesh,
And may not these two couple without scratching?

ÆCIUS
Alas, my noble friend.

MAXIMUS
Alas not me,
I am not wretched, for there's no man miserable
But he that makes himself so.

ÆCIUS
Will ye walk yet?

MAXIMUS
Come, come, she dare not dye, friend, that's the truth on't,
She knows the inticing sweets and delicacies
Of a young Princes pleasures, and I thank her,

She has made a way for Maximus to rise by.
Will't not become me bravely? why do you think
She wept, and said she was ravish'd? keep it here
And I'll discover to you.

ÆCIUS
Well.

MAXIMUS
She knows
I love no bitten flesh, and out of that hope
She might be from me, she contriv'd this knavery;
Was it not monstrous, friend?

ÆCIUS
Does he but seem so,
Or is he mad indeed?

MAXIMUS
Oh gods, my heart!

ÆCIUS
Would it would fairly break.

MAXIMUS
Methinks I am somewhat wilder than I was,
And yet I thank the gods I know my duty.

[Enter **CLAUDIA**.

CLAUDIA
Nay, you may spare your tears; she's dead.
She is so.

MAXIMUS
Why, so it should be: how?

CLAUDIA
When first she enter'd
Into her house, after a world of weeping,
And blushing like the Sun-set, as we see her;
Dare I, said she, defile this house with Whore,
In which his noble Family has flourish'd?
At which she fell, and stir'd no more; we rub'd her.

[Exit **CLAUDIA**.

MAXIMUS

No more of that; be gone; now my Æcius,
If thou wilt do me pleasure, weep a little,
I am so parch'd I cannot: Your example
Has brought the rain down now: now lead me friend,
And as we walk together, let's pray together truly,
I may not fall from faith.

ÆCIUS
That's nobly spoken.

MAXIMUS
Was I not wild, Æcius?

ÆCIUS
Somewhat troubled.

MAXIMUS
I felt no sorrow then; Now I'll go with ye,
But do not name the Woman; fye, what fool
Am I to weep thus? Gods, Lucina, take thee,
For thou wert even the best and worthiest Lady.

ÆCIUS
Good Sir, no more, I shall be melted with it.

MAXIMUS
I have done, and good Sir comfort me;
Would there were wars now.

ÆCIUS
Settle your thoughts, come.

MAXIMUS
So I have now, friend,
Of my deep lamentations here's an end.

[Exeunt.

SCÆNA SECUNDA

Enter **PONTIUS**, **PHIDIAS** and **ARETUS**.

PHIDIAS
By my faith, Captain Pontius, besides pity
Of your faln fortunes, what to say I know not,
For 'tis too true the Emperour desires not,

But my best master, any souldier near him.

ARETUS
And when he understands, he cast your fortunes
For disobedience, how can we incline him,
(That are but under persons to his favours)
To any fair opinion? Can ye sing?

PONTIUS
Not to please him, Aretus, for my Songs
Go not to th' Lute, or Viol, but to th' Trumpet,
My tune kept on a Target, and my subject
The well struck wounds of men, not love, or women.

PHIDIAS
And those he understands not.

PONTIUS
He should, Phidias.

ARETUS
Could you not leave this killing way a little?
You must, if here you would plant your self, and rather
Learn as we do, to like what those affect
That are above us; wear their actions,
And think they keep us warm too; what they say,
Though oftentimes they speak a little foolishly,
Not stay to construe, but prepare to execute,
And think however the end falls, the business
Cannot run empty handed.

PHIDIAS
Can ye flatter,
And if it were put to you, lye a little?

PONTIUS
Yes, if it be a living.

ARETUS
That's well said then.

PONTIUS
But must these lies and flatteries be believ'd then?

PHIDIAS
Oh yes, by any means.

PONTIUS

By any means then
I cannot lie nor flatter.

ARETUS
Ye must swear too,
If ye be there.

PONTIUS
I can swear if they move me.

PHIDIAS
Cannot ye forswear too?

PONTIUS
The Court for ever,
If it be grown so wicked.

ARETUS
You should procure a little too.

PONTIUS
What's that?
Mens honest sayings for my truth?

ARETUS
Oh no, Sir;
But womens honest actions for your trial.

PONTIUS
Do you do all these things?

PHIDIAS
Do you not like 'em?

PONTIUS
Do you ask me seriously, or trifle with me?
I am not so low yet to be your mirth.

ARETUS
You do mistake us, Captain, for sincerely,
We ask you how you like 'em?

PONTIUS
Then sincerely,
I tell ye I abhor 'em; they are ill ways,
And I will starve before I fall into 'em,
The doers of 'em Wretches, their base hungers
Care not whose Bread they eat, nor how they get it.

ARETUS
What then, Sir?

PONTIUS
If you profess this wickedness,
Because ye have been Souldiers, and born Arms,
The Servants of the brave Æcius,
And by him put to th' Emperour, give me leave,
Or I must take it else, to say ye are Villains,
For all your Golden Coats, debosh'd, base Villains,
Yet I do wear a Sword to tell you so,
Is this the way you mark out for a Souldier,
A Man that has commanded for the Empire,
And born the Reputation of a Man?
Are there not lazie things enough call'd fools and cowards,
And poor enough to be prefer'd for Panders,
But wanting Souldiers must be Knaves too? ha!
This the trim course of life; were not ye born Bawds,
And so inherit but your Rights? I am poor,
And may expect a worse; yet digging, pruning,
Mending of broken ways, carrying of water,
Planting of Worts and Onions, any thing
That's honest, and a Mans, I'll rather chuse,
I, and live better on it, which is juster,
Drink my well gotten water with more pleasure,
When my endeavours done, and wages paid me,
Than you do wine, eat my course Bread, not curst,
And mend upon't, your diets are diseases,
And sleep as soundly, when my labour bids me,
As any forward Pander of ye all,
And rise a great deal honester; my Garments,
Though not as yours, the soft sins of the Empire,
Yet may be warm, and keep the biting wind out,
When every single breath of poor opinion
Finds you through all your Velvets.

Put us good men to th' Emperour, so we have serv'd him,
Though much neglected for it; So dare be still;
Your Curses are not ours; we have seen your fortune,
But yet know no way to redeem it: Means,
Such as we have, ye shall not want, brave Pontius,
But pray be temperate, if we can wipe out
The way of your offences, we are yours, Sir;
And you shall live at Court an honest Man too.

PHIDIAS
That little meat and means we have, we'll share it,

Fear not to be as we are; what we told ye,
Were but meer tryals of your truth: y'are worthy,
And so we'll ever hold ye; suffer better,
And then you are a right Man, Pontius,
If my good Master be not ever angry,
Ye shall command again.

PONTIUS
I have found two good men: use my life,
For it is yours, and all I have to thank ye—

[Exeunt.

SCÆNA TERTIA

Enter **MAXIMUS**.

MAXIMUS
There's no way else to do it, he must dye,
This friend must dye, this soul of Maximus,
Without whom I am nothing but my shame,
This perfectness that keeps me from opinion,
Must dye, or I must live thus branded ever:
A hard choice, and a fatal; Gods ye have given me
A way to credit, but the ground to go on,
Ye have levell'd with that precious life I love most,
Yet I must on, and through, for if I offer
To take my way without him, like a Sea
He bears his high Command 'twixt me and vengeance,
And in mine own road sinks me, he is honest,
Of a most constant loyalty to Cæsar,
And when he shall but doubt, I dare attempt him,
But make a question of his ill, but say
What is a Cæsar, that he dare do this,
Dead sure he cuts me off; Æcius dyes,
Or I have lost my self: why should I kill him?
Why should I kill my self? for 'tis my killing,
Æcius is my root, and wither him,
Like a decaying Branch I fall to nothing.
Is he not more to me than Wife, than Cæsar?
Though I had now my safe revenge upon him,
Is he not more than rumour, and his friendship
Sweeter than the love of women? what is honour
We all so strangely are bewitch'd withal?
Can it relieve me if I want? he has;
Can honour 'twixt the incensed Prince and Envy,

Bear up the lives of worthy men? he has;
Can honour pull the wings of fearful Cowards,
And make 'em turn again like Tigers? he has;
And I have liv'd to see this, and preserv'd so:
Why should this empty word incite me then
To what is ill and cruel? let her perish.
A friend is more than all the world, than honour;
She is a woman and her loss the less,
And with her go my griefs; but hark ye Maximus,
Was she not yours? Did she not dye to tell ye
She was a ravish'd woman? Did not Justice
Nobly begin with her that not deserv'd it,
And shall he live that did it? Stay a little,
Can this abuse dye here? Shall not mens tongues
Dispute it afterward, and say I gave
(Affecting dull obedience, and tame duty,
And led away with fondness of a friendship)
The only vertue of the world to slander?
Is not this certain, was not she a chaste one,
And such a one, that no compare dwelt with her,
One of so sweet a vertue that Æcius,
Even he himself, this friend that holds me from it,
Out of his worthy love to me, and justice,
Had it not been on Cæsar, had reveng'd her?
He told me so; what shall I do then?

[Enter a **SERVANT**.

Can other men affect it, and I cold?
I fear he must not live.

SERVANT
My Lord, the General
Is come to seek ye.

MAXIMUS
Go, entreat him to enter;
O brave Æcius, I could wish thee now
As far from friendship to me, as from fears,
That I might cut thee off, like that I weigh'd not,
Is there no way without him to come near it?
For out of honesty he must destroy me
If I attempt it, he must dye as others,
And I must lose him; 'tis necessity,
Only the time and means is the difference;
But yet I would not make a murther of him,
Take him directly for my doubts; he shall dye,
I have found a way to do it, and a safe one,

It shall be honour to him too: I know not
What to determine certain, I am so troubled,
And such a deal of conscience presses me;

[Enter **ÆCIUS**.

Would I were dead my self.

ÆCIUS
You run away well;
How got you from me, friend?

MAXIMUS
That that leads mad men,
A strong imagination made me wander.

ÆCIUS
I thought you had been more setled.

MAXIMUS
I am well,
But you must give me leave a little sometimes
To have a buzzing in my brains.

ÆCIUS
Ye are dangerous,
But I'll prevent it if I can; ye told me
You would go to th' Army.

MAXIMUS
Why, to have my throat cut?
Must he not be the bravest man, Æcius,
That strikes me first?

ÆCIUS
You promised me a freedom
From all these thoughts, and why should any strike you?

MAXIMUS
I am an Enemy, a wicked one,
Worse than the foes of Rome, I am a Coward,
A Cuckold, and a Coward, that's two causes
Why every one should beat me.

ÆCIUS
Ye are neither;
And durst another tell me so, he dyed for't,
For thus far on mine honour, I'le assure you

No man more lov'd than you, and for your valour,
And what ye may be, fair; no man more follow'd.

MAXIMUS
A doughty man indeed: but that's all one,
The Emperour nor all the Princes living
Shall find a flaw in my Coat; I have suffer'd,
And can yet; let them find inflictions,
I'le find a body for 'em, or I'le break it.
'Tis not a Wife can thrust me out, some look't for't;
But let 'em look till they are blind with looking,
They are but fools; yet there is anger in me,
That I would fain disperse, and now I think on't,
You told me, friend, the Provinces are stirring,
We shall have sport I hope then, and what's dangerous,
A Battle shall beat from me.

ÆCIUS
Why do ye eye me,
With such a setled look?

MAXIMUS
Pray tell me this,
Do we not love extreamly? I love you so.

ÆCIUS
If I should say I lov'd not you as truly,
I should do that I never durst do, lye.

MAXIMUS
If I should dye, would it not grieve you much?

ÆCIUS
Without all doubt.

MAXIMUS
And could you live without me?

ÆCIUS
It would much trouble me to live without ye.
Our loves, and loving souls have been so us'd
But to one houshold in us: but to dye
Because I could not make you live, were woman,
Far much too weak, were it to save your worth,
Or to redeem your name from rooting out,
To quit you bravely fighting from the foe,
Or fetch ye off, where honour had ingag'd ye.
I ought, and would dye for ye.

MAXIMUS
Truly spoken.
What beast but I, that must, could hurt this man now?
Would he had ravish'd me, I would have paid him,
I would have taught him such a trick, his Eunuchs
Nor all his black-eyed Boys dreamt of yet;
By all the Gods I am mad now; now were Cæsar
Within my reach, and on his glorious top
The pile of all the world, he went to nothing;
The Destinies, nor all the dames of Hell,
Were I once grappl'd with him, should relieve him,
No not the hope of mankind more; all perished;
But this is words, and weakness.

ÆCIUS
Ye look strangely.

MAXIMUS
I look but as I am, I am a stranger.

ÆCIUS
To me?

MAXIMUS
To every one, I am no Roman;
Nor what I am do I know.

ÆCIUS
Then I'le leave ye.

MAXIMUS
I find I am best so, if ye meet with Maximus
Pray bid him be an honest man for my sake,
You may do much upon him; for his shadow,
Let me alone.

ÆCIUS
Ye were not wont to talk thus,
And to your friend; ye have some danger in you,
That willingly would run to action,
Take heed, by all our love take heed.

MAXIMUS
I danger?
I, willing to do any thing, I dig.
Has not my Wife been dead two dayes already?
Are not my mournings by this time moth-eaten?

Are not her sins dispers'd to other Women,
And many one ravish'd to relieve her?
Have I shed tears these twelve hours?

ÆCIUS
Now ye weep.

MAXIMUS
Some lazie drops that staid behind.

ÆCIUS
I'le tell ye
And I must tell ye truth, were it not hazard,
And almost certain loss of all the Empire,
I would join with ye: were it any mans
But his life, that is life of us, he lost it
For doing of this mischief: I would take it,
And to your rest give ye a brave revenge:
But as the rule now stands, and as he rules,
And as the Nations hold in disobedience,
One pillar failing, all must fall; I dare not:
Nor is it just you should be suffer'd in it,
Therefore again take heed: On forraign foes
We are our own revengers, but at home
On Princes that are eminent and ours,
'Tis fit the Gods should judge us: be not rash,
Nor let your angry steel cut those ye know not,
For by this fatal blow, if ye dare strike it,
As I see great aims in ye, those unborn yet,
And those to come of them, and these succeeding
Shall bleed the wrath of Maximus: for me
As ye now bear your self, I am your friend still,
If ye fall off I will not flatter ye,
And in my hands, were ye my soul, you perish'd:
Once more be careful, stand, and still be worthy,
I'le leave you for this hour.

[Exit.

MAXIMUS
Pray do, 'tis done:
And friendship, since thou canst not hold in dangers,
Give me a certain ruin, I must through it.

[Exit.

Enter **EMPEROUR**, **LICINIUS**, **CHILAX** and **BALBUS**.

EMPEROUR
Dead?

CHILAX
So 'tis thought, Sir.

EMPEROUR
How?

LICINIUS
Grief, and disgrace,
As people say.

EMPEROUR
No more, I have too much on't,
Too much by you, you whetters of my follies,
Ye Angel formers of my sins, but Devils;
Where is your cunning now? you would work wonders,
There was no chastity above your practice,
You would undertake to make her love her wrongs,
And doate upon her rape: mark what I tell ye,
If she be dead—

CHILAX
Alas Sir.

EMPEROUR
Hang ye Rascals,
Ye blasters of my youth, if she be gone,
'Twere better ye had been your Fathers Camels,
Groan'd under daily weights of wood and water:
Am I not Cæsar?

LICINIUS
Mighty and our Maker.

EMPEROUR
Than thus have given my pleasures to destruction.
Look she be living, slaves.

LICINIUS
We are no Gods Sir,

If she be dead, to make her new again.

EMPEROUR

She cannot dye, she must not dye; are those
I plant my love upon but common livers?
Their hours as others, told 'em? can they be ashes?
Why do ye flatter a belief into me
That I am all that is, the world's my creature,
The Trees bring forth their fruits when I say Summer,
The Wind that knows no limit but his wildness,
At my command moves not a leaf; the Sea
With his proud mountain waters envying Heaven,
When I say still, run into Crystal mirrors,
Can I do this and she dye? Why ye bubbles
That with my least breath break, no more remembred;
Ye moths that fly about my flame and perish,
Ye golden canker-worms, that eat my honours,
Living no longer than my spring of favour:
Why do ye make me God that can do nothing?
Is she not dead?

CHILAX

All Women are not with her.

EMPEROUR

A common Whore serves you, and far above ye,
The pleasures of a body lam'd with lewdness;
A meer perpetual motion makes ye happy;
Am I a man to traffick with Diseases?
Can any but a chastity serve Cæsar?
And such a one that Gods would kneel to purchase?
You think because you have bred me up to pleasures,
And almost run me over all the rare ones,
Your Wives will serve the turn: I care not for 'em,
Your Wives are Fencers Whores, and shall be Footmens,
Though sometimes my nice will, or rather anger
Have made ye Cuckolds for variety;
I would not have ye hope, nor dream ye poor ones
Alwaies so great a blessing from me; go
Get your own infamy hereafter Rascals,
I have done too nobly for ye, ye enjoy
Each one an heir, the Royal seed of Cæsar,
And I may curse ye for't; your wanton Gennets
That are so proud, the wind get's 'em with fillies,
Taught me this foul intemperance: Thou Licinius
Hast such a Messalina, such a Lais,
The backs of Bulls cannot content, nor Stallions,
The sweat of fifty men a night do's nothing.

LICINIUS
Your Grace but jests I hope.

EMPEROUR
'Tis Oracle.
The sins of other Women put by hers
Shew off like sanctities: Thine's a fool, Chilax,
Yet she can tell to twenty, and all lovers,
And all lien with her too, and all as she is,
Rotten, and ready for an Hospital.
Yours is an holy Whore, friend Balbus.

BALBUS
Well Sir.

EMPEROUR
One that can pray away the sins she suffers,
But not the punishments: she has had ten Bastards,
Five of 'em now are Lictors, yet she prayes;
She has been the Song of Rome, and common Pasquil;
Since I durst see a Wench, she was Camp Mistris,
And muster'd all the cohorts, paid 'em too,
They have it yet to shew, and yet she prayes;
She is now to enter old men that are Children,
And have forgot their rudiments: am I
Left for these withered vices? and but one,
But one of all the world that could content me,
And snatch'd away in shewing? If your Wives
Be not yet Witches, or your selves now be so
And save your lives, raise me this noble beauty
As when I forc'd her, full of constancy,
Or by the Gods—

LICINIUS
Most sacred Cæsar.

EMPEROUR
Slaves.

[Enter **PROCULUS**.

LICINIUS
Good Proculus.

PROCULUS
You shall not see it,
It may concern the Empire.

EMPEROUR

Ha: what said'st thou?
Is she not dead?

PROCULUS

Not any one I know, Sir;
I come to bring your Grace a Letter, here
Scatter'd belike i'th' Court: 'tis sent to Maximus
And bearing danger in it.

EMPEROUR

Danger? where?
Double our Guard.

PROCULUS

Nay no where, but i'th' Letter.

EMPEROUR

What an afflicted Conscience do I live with,
And what a beast I am grown! I had forgotten
To ask Heaven mercy for my fault, and was now
Even ravishing again her memory,
I find there must be danger in this deed:
Why do I stand disputing then and whining?
For what is not the gods to give, they cannot
Though they would link their powers in one, do mischief.
This Letter may betray me, get ye gone

[Exeunt.

And wait me in the Garden, guard the house well,
And keep this from the Empress: the name Maximus
Runs through me like a feavour, this may be
Some private Letter upon private business,
Nothing concerning me: why should I open't?
I have done him wrong enough already; yet
It may concern me too, the time so tells me;
The wicked deed I have done, assures me 'tis so.
Be what it will, I'le see it, if that be not
Part of my fears, among my other sins,
I'le purge it out in prayers:
How? what's this?
Letter read] Lord Maximus, you love Æcius,
And are his noble friend too; bid him be less,
I mean less with the people, times are dangerous:
The Army's his, the Emperour in doubts;
And as some will not stick to say, declining,

You stand a constant man in either fortune;
Perswade him, he is lost else: Though ambition
Be the last sin he touches at, or never;
Yet what the people mad with loving him,
And as they willingly desire another
May tempt him to, or rather force his goodness,
Is to be doubted mainly: he is all,
(As he stands now) but the meer name of Cæsar,
And should the Emperour inforce him lesser,
Not coming from himself, it were more dangerous:
He is honest, and will hear you: doubts are scatter'd,
And almost come to growth in every houshold:
Yet in my foolish judgment, were this master'd,
The people that are now but rage, and his,
Might be again obedience: you shall know me
When Rome is fair again; till when I love you.
No name! this may be cunning, yet it seems not;
For there is nothing in it but is certain,
Besides my safety.
Had not good Germanicus,
That was as loyal, and as straight as he is,
If not prevented by Tiberius,
Been by the Souldiers forc'd their Emperour?
He had, and 'tis my wisdom to remember it.
And was not Corbulo, even that Corbulo,
That ever fortunate and living Roman,
That broke the heart-strings of the Parthians,
And brought Arsaces line upon their knees,
Chain'd to the awe of Rome, because he was thought
(And but in wine once) fit to make a Cæsar,
Cut off by Nero? I must seek my safety:
For 'tis the same again, if not beyond it:
I know the Souldier loves him more than Heaven,
And will adventure all his gods to raise him;
Me he hates more than peace: what this may breed,
If dull security and confidence
Let him grow up, a fool may find and laught at.
But why Lord Maximus I injur'd so,
Should be the man to counsel him, I know not;
More than he has been friend, and lov'd allegeance:
What now he is I fear, for his abuses
Without the people dare draw blood; who waits there?

[Enter a **SERVANT**.

SERVANT
Your Grace.

EMPEROUR
Call Phidias and Aretus hither:
I'le find a day for him too; times are dangerous,
The Army his, the Emperour in doubts:
I find it is too true; did he not tell me
1. As if he had intent to make me odious,
2. And to my face; and by a way of terror,
What vices I was grounded in, and almost
Proclaim'd the Souldiers hate against me? is not
The sacred name and dignity of Cæsar
(Were this Æcius more than man) sufficient
To shake off all his honesty? He's dangerous
Though he be good, and though a friend, a fear'd one,
And such I must not sleep by: are they come yet?
I do believe this fellow, and I thank him;
'Twas time to look about, if I must perish,
Yet shall my fears go formost.

[Enter **PHIDIAS** and **ARETUS**.

PHIDIAS
Life to Cæsar.

EMPEROUR
Is Lord Æcius waiting?

PHIDIAS
Not this morning,
I rather think he's with the Army.

EMPEROUR
Army?
I do not like that Army: go unto him,
And bid him straight attend me, and do ye hear,
Come private without any; I have business
Only for him.

PHIDIAS
Your Graces pleasure—

[Exit **PHIDIAS**.

EMPEROUR
Go;
What Souldier is the same, I have seen him often,
That keeps you company, Aretus?

ARETUS

Me Sir?

EMPEROUR
I you, Sir.

ARETUS
One they call Pontius,
And't please your Grace.

EMPEROUR
A Captain?

ARETUS
Yes, he was so;
But speaking something roughly in his want,
Especially of Wars, the Noble General
Out of strict allegiance cast his fortunes.

EMPEROUR
H'as been a valiant fellow.

ARETUS
So he's still.

EMPEROUR
Alas, the General might have pardon'd follies,
Souldiers will talk sometimes.

ARETUS
I am glad of this.

EMPEROUR
He wants preferment as I take it.

ARETUS
Yes Sir;
And for that noble Grace his life shall serve.

EMPEROUR
I have a service for him:
I shame a Souldier should become a Begger:
I like the man Aretus.

ARETUS
Gods protect ye.

EMPEROUR
Bid him repair to Proculus, and there

He shall receive the business, and reward for't:
I'le see him setled too, and as a Souldier,
We shall want such.

ARETUS
The sweets of Heaven still crown ye.

EMPEROUR
I have a fearful darkness in my soul,
And till I be deliver'd, still am dying.

[Exeunt.

SCÆNA SECUNDA

Enter **MAXIMUS** alone.

MAXIMUS
My way has taken: all the Court's in guard,
And business every where, and every corner
Full of strange whispers: I am least in rumour,

[Enter **ÆCIUS** and **PHIDIAS**.

And so I'le keep my self. Here comes Æcius,
I see the bait is swallow'd: If he be lost
He is my Martyr, and my way stands open,
And honour on thy head, his blood is reckon'd.

ÆCIUS
Why how now friend, what makes ye here unarm'd?
Are ye turn'd Merchant?

MAXIMUS
By your fair perswasions,
And such a Merchant trafficks without danger;
I have forgotten all, Æcius,
And which is more, forgiven.

ÆCIUS
Now I love ye,
Truly I do, ye are a worthy Roman.

MAXIMUS
The fair repentance of my Prince to me
Is more than sacrifice of bloud and vengeance,

No eyes shall weep her ruins, but mine own.

ÆCIUS
Still ye take more love from me: vertuous friend
The gods make poor Aecius worthy of thee.

MAXIMUS
Only in me y'are poor Sir: and I worthy
Only in being yours:
But why your arm thus,
Have ye been hurt Aecius?

ÆCIUS
Bruis'd a little:
My horse fell with me friend: which till this morning
I never knew him do.

MAXIMUS
Pray gods it boad well;
And now I think on't better, ye shall back,
Let my perswasions rule ye.

ÆCIUS
Back, why Maximus?
The Emperour commands me come.

MAXIMUS
I like not
At this time his command.

ÆCIUS
I do at all times,
And all times will obey it, why not now then?

MAXIMUS
I'le tell ye why, and as I have been govern'd,
Be you so, noble friend: The Court's in Guard,
Arm'd strongly, for what purpose, let me fear;
I do not like your going.

ÆCIUS
Were it fire;
And that fire certain to consume this body,
If Cæsar sent, I would goe; never fear man,
If he take me, he takes his arms away,
I am too plain and true to be suspected.

MAXIMUS

Then I have dealt unwisely.

ÆCIUS
If the Emperour,
Because he meerely may, will have my life,
That's all he has to work on, and all shall have:
Let him, he loves me better: here I wither,
And happily may live, till ignorantly
I run into a fault worth death: nay more, dishonour.
Now all my sins, I dare say those of duty
Are printed here, and if I fall so happy,
I bless the grave I lye in, and the gods
Equal, as dying on the Enemy,
Must take me up a Sacrifice.

MAXIMUS
Goe on then,
And I'le goe with ye.

ÆCIUS
No, ye may not friend.

MAXIMUS
He cannot be a friend, bars me Aecius,
Shall I forsake ye in my doubts?

ÆCIUS
Ye must.

MAXIMUS
I must not, nor I will not; have I liv'd
Only to be a Carpet friend for pleasure?
I can endure a death as well as Cato.

ÆCIUS
There is no death nor danger in my going,
Nor none must goe along.

MAXIMUS
I have a sword too,
And once I could have us'd it for my friend.

ÆCIUS
I need no sword, nor friend in this, pray leave me;
And as ye love me, do not overlove me;
I am commanded none shall come: at supper
I'le meet ye, and weel drink a cup or two,
Ye need good Wine, ye have been sad: Farewel.

MAXIMUS
Farewel my noble friend, let me embrace ye
E're ye depart; it may be one of us
Shall never do the like again.

ÆCIUS
Yes often.

MAXIMUS
Farewel good dear Aecius.

ÆCIUS
Farewel Maximus
Till night: indeed you doubt too much.—

[Exit.

MAXIMUS
I do not:
Goe worthy innocent, and make the number
Of Cæsars sins so great, Heaven may want mercy:
I'le hover hereabout to know what passes:
And if he be so devilish to destroy thee,
In thy bloud shall begin his Tragedy.—

[Exit.

SCÆNA TERTIA

Enter **PROCULUS** and **PONTIUS**.

PROCULUS
Besides this, if you do it, you enjoy
The noble name Patrician: more than that too,
The friend of Cæsar ye are stil'd: there's nothing
Within the hopes of Rome, or present being,
But you may safely say is yours.

PONTIUS
Pray stay Sir;
What has Aecius done to be destroy'd?
At least I would have a colour.

PROCULUS
Ye have more,

Nay all that may be given, he is a Traitor,
One, any man would strike that were a subject.

PONTIUS
Is he so foul?

PROCULUS
Yes, a most fearfull Traytor.

PONTIUS
A fearfull plague upon thee, for thou lyest;
I ever thought the Souldier would undoe him
With his too much affection.

PROCULUS
Ye have hit it,
They have brought him to ambition.

PONTIUS
Then he is gone.

PROCULUS
The Emperour out of a foolish pitie,
Would save him yet.

PONTIUS
Is he so mad?

PROCULUS
He's madder!
Would goe to'th' Army to him.

PONTIUS
Would he so?

PROCULUS
Yes Pontius; but we consider—

PONTIUS
Wisely.

PROCULUS
How else man, that the state lies in it.

PONTIUS
And your lives too.

PROCULUS

And every mans.

PONTIUS
He did me
All the disgrace he could.

PROCULUS
And scurvily.

PONTIUS
Out of a mischief meerly: did you mark it?

PROCULUS
Yes well enough.
Now ye have means to quit it,
The deed done, take his place.

PONTIUS
Pray let me think on't,
'Tis ten to one I do it.

PROCULUS
Do and be happy.—

[Exit **PROCULUS**.

PONTIUS
This Emperour is made of nought but mischief,
Sure, Murther was his Mother: none to lop,
But the main link he had? upon my conscience
The man is truly honest, and that kills him;
For to live here, and study to be true,
Is all one to be Traitors: why should he die?
Have they not Slaves and Rascals for their Offrings
In full abundance; Bawds more than beasts for slaughter?
Have they not singing whores enough, and knaves too,
And millions of such Martyrs to sink Charon,
But the best sons of Rome must sail too? I will shew him
(since he must dye) a way to do it truly:
And though he bears me hard, yet shall he know,
I am born to make him bless me for a blow.—

[Exit.

SCÆNA QUARTA

Enter **PHIDIAS**, **ARETUS**, and **ÆCIUS**.

PHIDIAS
Yet ye may 'scape to th' Camp, we'l hazard with ye.

ARETUS
Lose not your life so basely Sir: ye are arm'd,
And many when they see your sword out, and know why,
Must follow your adventure.

ÆCIUS
Get ye from me:
Is not the doom of Cæsar on this body,
Do not I bear my last hour here, now sent me?
Am I not old Aecius, ever dying?
You think this tenderness and love you bring me,
'Tis treason, and the strength of disobedience,
And if ye tempt me further, ye shall feel it:
I seek the Camp for safety, when my death
Ten times more glorious than my life, and lasting
Bids me be happy? Let the fool fear dying,
Or he that weds a woman for his honour,
Dreaming no other life to come but kisses;
Aecius is not now to learn to suffer:
If ye dare shew a just affection, kill me,
I stay but those that must: why do ye weep?
Am I so wretched to deserve mens pities?
Goe give your tears to those that lose their worths,
Bewail their miseries, for me wear Garlands,
Drink wine, and much; sing Peans to my praise,
I am to triumph friends, and more than Cæsar,
For Cæsar fears to die, I love to die.

PHIDIAS
O my dear Lord!

ÆCIUS
No more, goe, goe I say;
Shew me not signs of sorrow, I deserve none:
Dare any man lament, I should die nobly?
Am I grown old to have such enemies?
When I am dead, speak honourably of me,
That is, preserve my memory from dying;
There if you needs must weep your ruin'd Master,
A tear or two will seem well: this I charge ye,
(because ye say you yet love old Aecius)
See my poor body burnt, and some to sing
About my Pile, and what I have done and suffer'd,

If Cæsar kill not that too: at your banquets
When I am gone, if any chance to number
The times that have been sad and dangerous,
Say how I fell, and 'tis sufficient:
No more I say, he that laments my end
By all the gods dishonours me; be gone
And suddainly, and wisely from my dangers,
My death is catching else.

PHIDIAS
We fear not dying.

ÆCIUS
Yet fear a wilfull death, the just Gods hate it,
I need no company to that that Children
Dare do alone, and Slaves are proud to purchase;
Live till your honesties, as mine has done,
Make this corrupted age sick of your vertues,
Then dye a sacrifice, and then ye know
The noble use of dying well, and Roman.

ARETUS
And must we leave ye Sir?

ÆCIUS
We must all die,
All leave our selves, it matters not where, when,
Nor how, so we die well: and can that man that does so
Need lamentation for him? Children weep
Because they have offended, or for fear;
Women for want of will, and anger; is there
In noble man, that truly feels both poyses
Of life and death, so much of this wet weakness,
To drown a glorious death in child and woman?
I am asham'd to see ye; yet ye move me,
And were it not my manhood would accuse me,
For covetous to live, I should weep with ye.

PHIDIAS
O we shall never see you more.

ÆCIUS
'Tis true;
Nor I the miseries that Rome shall suffer,
Which is a benefit life cannot reckon:
But what I have been, which is just, and faithfull;
One that grew old for Rome, when Rome forgot him,
And for he was an honest man durst die,

Ye shall have daily with ye: could that dye too,
And I return no traffick of my travels,
No pay to have been Souldier, but this Silver,
No Annals of Æcius, but he liv'd,
My friends, ye had cause to weep, and bitterly;
The common overflows of tender women,
And children new born crying, were too little
To shew me then most wretched: if tears must be,
I should in justice weep 'em, and for you,
You are to live, and yet behold those slaughters
The drie, and wither'd bones of death would bleed at:
But sooner, than I have time to think what must be,
I fear you'l find what shall be;
If ye love me,
Let that word serve for all, be gone and leave me;
I have some little practice with my soul,
And then the sharpest sword is welcom'st; goe,
Pray be gone, ye have obey'd me living,
Be not for shame now stubborn; so I thank ye,
And fare ye well, a better fortune guide ye—

[Exeunt **PHIDIAS** and **ARETUS**.

I am a little thirstie, not for fear,
And yet it is a kind of fear, I say so;
Is it to be a just man now again,
And leave my flesh unthought of? 'tis departed:
I hear 'em come, who strikes first?
I stay for ye:

[Enter **BALBUS**, **CHILAX**, **LICINIUS**.

Yet I will dye a Souldier, my sword drawn,
But against none:
Why do ye fear? come forward.

BALBUS
You were a Souldier Chilax.

CHILAX
Yes, I muster'd
But never saw the Enemy.

LICINIUS
He's drawn,
By heaven I dare not do it.

ÆCIUS

Why do ye tremble?
I am to die, come ye not now from Cæsar
To that end, speak?

BALBUS
We do, and we must kill ye,
'Tis Cæsars will.

CHILAX
I charge you put your sword up,
That we may do it handsomly.

ÆCIUS
Ha, ha, ha,
My sword up, handsomly? where were ye bred?
Ye are the merriest murderers my masters
I ever met withal; Come forward fools,
Why do ye stare? upon mine honour Bawds,
I will not strike ye.

LICINIUS
I'le not be first.

BALBUS
Nor I.

CHILAX
You had best die quietly: the Emperour
Sees how you bear your self.

ÆCIUS
I would die Rascals,
If you would kill me quietly.

BALBUS
—of Proculus,
He promis'd us to bring a Captain hither,
That has been used to kill.

ÆCIUS
I'le call the Guard,
Unless you will kill me quickly, and proclaim
What beastly, base, and cowardly companions
The Emperour has trusted with his safetie:
Nay I'le give out, ye fell of my side, villains,
Strike home ye bawdy slaves.

CHILAX

He will kill us,
I mark'd his hand, he waits but time to reach us,
Now do you offer.

ÆCIUS
If ye do mangle me,
And kill me not at two blows, or at three,
Or not so stagger me, my senses fail me,
Look to your selves.

CHILAX
I told ye.

ÆCIUS
Strike me manly,
And take a thousand strokes.—

[Enter **PONTIUS**.

BALBUS
Here's Pontius.

PONTIUS
Not kill'd him yet?
Is this the love ye bear the Emperour?
Nay then I see ye are Traitors all, have at ye.—

[**LICINIUS** runs away.

CHILAX
Oh I am hurt.

BALBUS
And I am kill'd—

[Exeunt **CHILAX** and **BALBUS**.

PONTIUS
Dye Bawds;
As ye have liv'd and flourish'd.

ÆCIUS
Wretched fellow,
What hast thou done?

PONTIUS
Kill'd them that durst not kill,
And you are next.

ÆCIUS
Art thou not Pontius?

PONTIUS
I am the same you cast Æcius,
And in the face of all the Camp disgrac'd.

ÆCIUS
Then so much nobler, as thou wert a Souldier,
Shall my death be: is it revenge provok'd thee,
Or art thou hir'd to kill me?

PONTIUS
Both.

ÆCIUS
Then do it.

PONTIUS
Is that all?

ÆCIUS
Yes.

PONTIUS
Would you not live?

ÆCIUS
Why should I,
To thank thee for my life?

PONTIUS
Yes, if I spare it.

ÆCIUS
Be not deceiv'd, I was not made to thank
For any courtesie, but killing me,
A fellow of thy fortune; do thy duty.

PONTIUS
Do not you fear me?

ÆCIUS
No.

PONTIUS
Nor love me for it?

ÆCIUS
That's as thou dost thy business.

PONTIUS
When you are dead,
Your place is mine Æcius.

ÆCIUS
Now I fear thee,
And not alone thee Pontius, but the Empire.

PONTIUS
Why, I can govern Sir.

ÆCIUS
I would thou couldst,
And first thy self: Thou canst fight well, and bravely,
Thou canst endure all dangers, heats, colds, hungers;
Heavens angry flashes are not suddainer,
Than I have seen thee execute; nor more mortal;
The winged feet of flying enemies
I have stood and view'd thee mow away like rushes,
And still kill the killer: were thy minde,
But half so sweet in peace, as rough in dangers,
I died to leave a happy heir behind me;
Come strike, and be a General.

PONTIUS
Prepare then:
And, for I see your honour cannot lessen,
And 'twere a shame for me to strike a dead man,
Fight your short span out.

ÆCIUS
No thou knowst I must not,
I dare not give thee so much vantage of me,
As disobedience.

PONTIUS
Dare ye not defend ye
Against your enemy?

ÆCIUS
Not sent from Cæsar,
I have no power to make such enemies;
For as I am condemn'd, my naked sword
Stands but a hatchment by me; only held

To shew I was a Souldier; had not Cæsar
Chain'd all defence in this doom, let him die,
Old as I am, and quench'd with scarrs, and sorrows,
Yet would I make this wither'd Arm do wonders,
And open in an enemy such wounds
Mercy would weep to look on.

PONTIUS
Then have at ye,
And look upon me, and be sure ye fear not:
Remember who you are, and why you live,
And what I have been to you: cry not hold,
Nor think it base injustice I should kill ye.

ÆCIUS
I am prepar'd for all.

PONTIUS
For now Æcius,
Thou shalt behold and find I was no traitor,
And as I do it, bless me; die as I do.—

[**PONTIUS** kills himself.

ÆCIUS
Thou hast deceiv'd me Pontius, and I thank thee;
By all my hopes in Heaven, thou art a Roman.

PONTIUS
To shew you what you ought to do, this is not;
For slanders self would shame to find you coward,
Or willing to out-live your honestie:
But noble Sir, ye have been jealous of me,
And held me in the rank of dangerous persons,
And I must dying say it was but justice,
Ye cast me from my credit; yet believe me,
For there is nothing now but truth to save me,
And your forgiveness, though ye held me hainous,
And of a troubled spirit, that like fire
Turns all to flames it meets with, ye mistook me;
If I were foe to any thing, 'twas ease,
Want of the Souldiers due, the Enemy
The nakedness we found at home, and scorn,
Children of peace, and pleasures, no regard
Nor comfort for our scars, but how we got 'em,
To rusty time, that eat our bodies up,
And even began to prey upon our honours,
To wants at home, and more than wants, abuses,

To them, that when the Enemy invaded
Made us their Saints, but now the sores of Rome;
To silken flattery, and pride plain'd over,
Forgetting with what wind their feathers sail,
And under whose protection their soft pleasures
Grow full and numberless: to this I am foe,
Not to the state, or any point of duty:
And let me speak but what a Souldier may,
Truly I ought to be so; yet I err'd,
Because a far more noble sufferer
Shew'd me the way to patience, and I lost it:
This is the end I die Sir; to live basely,
And not the follower of him that bred me,
In full account and vertue, Pontius dare not,
Much less to out-live what is good, and flatter.

ÆCIUS
I want a name to give thy vertue Souldier,
For only good is far below thee Pontius,
The gods shall find thee one; thou hast fashion'd death
In such an excellent, and beauteous manner,
I wonder men can live: Canst thou speak once more,
For thy words are such harmony, a soul
Would choose to flye to Heaven in.

PONTIUS
A farewel:
Good noble General your hand, forgive me,
And think what ever was displeasing you,
Was none of mine: ye cannot live.

ÆCIUS
I will not:
Yet one word more.

PONTIUS
Dye nobly: Rome farewel:
And Valentinian fall, thou hast broke thy Basis.
In joy ye have given me a quiet death,
I would strike more wounds, if I had more breath—

[He dyes.

ÆCIUS
Is there an hour of goodness beyond this?
Or any man would out-live such a dying?
Would Cæsar double all my honours on me,
And stick me o're with favours, like a Mistris;

Yet would I grow to this man: I have loved,
But never doated on a face till now:
O death thou art more than beautie, and thy pleasure
Beyond posterity: Come friends and kill me;
Cæsar be kind, and send a thousand swords,
The more, the greater is my fall: why stay ye?
Come, and I'le kiss your weapons: fear me not,
By all the gods I'le honour ye for killing:
Appear, or through the Court, and world, I'le search ye:
My sword is gone; ye are Traitors if ye spare me,
And Cæsar must consume ye: all base cowards?
I'le follow ye, and e're I dye proclaim ye
The weeds of Italy; the dross of nature—
Where are ye, villains, traytors, slaves.—

[Exit.

[Enter **PROCULUS**, and **THREE OTHERS** running over the Stage.

PROCULUS
I knew
H'ad kill'd the Captain.

1ST PERSON
Here's his sword.

PROCULUS
Let it alone, 'twill fight it self else; friends,
An hundred men are not enough to do it,
I'le to the Emperour, and get more aid.

ÆCIUS
None strike a poor condemned man?

PROCULUS
He is mad:
Shift for your selves my Masters.—

[Exeunt.

[Enter **ÆCIUS**.

ÆCIUS
Then Æcius,
See what thou darst thy self; hold my good sword,
Thou hast been kept from bloud too long, I'le kiss thee,
For thou art more then friend now, my preserver,
Shew me the way to happiness, I seek it:

And all you great ones, that have faln as I do,
To keep your memories, and honours living,
Be present in your vertues, and assist me,
That like strong Cato, I may put away
All promises, but what shall crown my ashes;
Rome, fare thee well: stand long, and know to conquer
Whilst there is people, and ambition:
Now for a stroak shall turn me to a Star:
I come ye blessed spirits, make me room
To live for ever in Elyzium:
Do men fear this? O that posterity
Could learn from him but this, that loves his wound,
There is no pain at all in dying well,
Nor none are lost, but those that make their hell—

[Kills himself.

[Enter **PROCULUS**, and **TWO OTHERS**.

FIRST OTHER
He's dead, draw in the Guard again.

PROCULUS
He's dead indeed,
And I am glad he's gone; he was a Devil:
His body, if his Eunuchs come, is theirs;
The Emperour out of his love to vertue,
Has given 'em that: Let no man stop their entrance.

[Exeunt.

[Enter **PHIDIAS** and **ARETUS**.

PHIDIAS
O my most noble Lord, look here Aretus,
Here's a sad sight.

ARETUS
O cruelty! O Cæsar!
O times that bring forth nothing but destruction,
And overflows of bloud: why wast thou kill'd?
Is it to be a just man now again,
As when Tiberius and wild Nero reign'd,
Only assurance of his over throw?

PHIDIAS
It is Aretus: he that would live now,
Must like the Toad, feed only on corruptions,

And grow with those to greatness: honest vertue,
And the true Roman honour, faith and valour
That have been all the riches of the Empire,
Now like the fearfull tokens of the Plague,
Are meer fore-runners of their ends that owe 'em.

ARETUS
Never enough lamented Lord: dear Master—

[Enter **MAXIMUS**.

Of whom now shall we learn to live like men?
From whom draw out our actions just, and worthy?
Oh thou art gone, and gone with thee all goodness,
The great example of all equitie,
O thou alone a Roman, thou art perish'd,
Faith, fortitude, and constant nobleness,
Weep Rome, weep Italy, weep all that knew him,
And you that fear'd him as a noble Foe,
(If Enemies have honourable tears)
Weep this decay'd Æcius faln, and scattered—
By foul, and base suggestion.

PHIDIAS
O Lord Maximus,
This was your worthy friend.

MAXIMUS
The gods forgive me:
Think not the worse my friends, I shed not tears,
Great griefs lament within; yet now I have found 'em:
Would I had never known the world, nor women,
Nor what that cursed name of honour was,
So this were once again Æcius:
But I am destin'd to a mighty action,
And begg my pardon friend, my vengeance taken,
I will not be long from thee: ye have a great loss,
But bear it patiently, yet to say truth
In justice 'tis not sufferable: I am next,
And were it now, I would be glad on't: friends,
Who shall preserve you now?

ARETUS
Nay we are lost too.

MAXIMUS
I fear ye are, for likely such as love
The man that's faln, and have been nourish'd by him,

Do not stay long behind: 'Tis held no wisdom.
I know what I must do. O my Æcius,
Canst thou thus perish, pluckt up by the roots,
And no man feel thy worthiness? From boys
He bred you both I think.

PHIDIAS
And from the poorest.

MAXIMUS
And lov'd ye as his own.

ARETUS
We found it Sir.

MAXIMUS
Is not this a loss then?

PHIDIAS
O, a loss of losses;
Our lives, and ruines of our families,
The utter being nothing of our names,
Were nothing near it.

MAXIMUS
As I take it too,
He put ye to the Emperour.

ARETUS
He did so.

MAXIMUS
And kept ye still in credit.

PHIDIAS
'Tis most true Sir.

MAXIMUS
He fed your Fathers too, and made them means,
Your Sisters he prefer'd to noble Wedlocks,
Did he not friends?

ARETUS
Oh yes Sir.

MAXIMUS
As I take it
This worthy man would not be now forgotten,

I tell ye to my grief, he was basely murdred;
And something would be done, by those that lov'd him:
And something may be: pray stand off a little,
Let me bewail him private: O my dearest.

PHIDIAS
Aretus, if we be not sudden, he outdoes us,
I know he points at vengeance; we are cold,
And base ungratefull wretches, if we shun it:
Are we to hope for more rewards, or greatness,
Or any thing but death, now he is dead?
Dar'st thou resolve?

ARETUS
I am perfect.

PHIDIAS
Then like flowers
That grew together all we'l fall together,
And with us that that bore us: when 'tis done
The world shall stile us two deserving servants:
I fear he will be before us.

ARETUS
This night Phidias.

PHIDIAS
No more.

MAXIMUS
Now worthy friends I have done my mournings,
Let's burn this noble body: Sweets as many
As sun-burnt Meroe breeds, I'le make a flame of,
Shall reach his soul in Heaven: he that shall live
Ten ages hence, but to reherse this story,
Shall with the sad discourse on't, darken Heaven,
And force the painful burdens from the wombs
Conceiv'd a new with sorrow: even the Grave
Where mighty Sylla sleeps shall rend asunder
And give her shadow up, to come and groan
About our piles, which will be more, and greater
Than green Olympus, Ida, or old Latmus
Can feed with Cedar, or the East with Gums,
Greece with her wines, or Thessalie with flowers,
Or willing heaven can weep for in her showres.

[Exeunt.

ACTUS QUINTUS

SCÆNA PRIMA

Enter **PHIDIAS**, with his dagger in him, and **ARETUS**, poyson'd.

ARETUS
He has his last.

PHIDIAS
Then come the worst of danger,
Æcius to thy soul we give a Cæsar.
How long is't since ye gave it him?

ARETUS
An hour,
Mine own two hours before him: how it boils me!

PHIDIAS
It was not to be cur'd I hope.

ARETUS
No Phidias,
I dealt above his Antidotes: Physicians
May find the cause, but where the cure?

PHIDIAS
Done bravely,
We are got before his Tyranny Aretus.

ARETUS
We had lost our worthiest end else Phidias.

PHIDIAS
Canst thou hold out a while?

ARETUS
To torture him
Anger would give me leave, to live an age yet;
That man is poorly spirited, whose life
Runs in his bloud alone, and not in's wishes,
And yet I swell, and burn like flaming Ætna,
A thousand new found fires are kindled in me,
But yet I must not die this four hours Phidias.

PHIDIAS

Remember who dies with thee, and despise death.

ARETUS
I need no exhortation, the joy in me
Of what I have done, and why, makes poyson pleasure,
And my most killing torments mistresses.
For how can he have time to dye, or pleasure
That falls as fools unsatisfied, and simple?

PHIDIAS
This that consumes my life, yet keeps it in me,
Nor do I feel the danger of a dying,
And if I but endure to hear the curses
Of this fell Tyrant dead, I have half my Heaven.

ARETUS
Hold thy soul fast but four hours Phidias,
And thou shalt see to wishes beyond ours,
Nay more beyond our meanings.

PHIDIAS
Thou hast steel'd me:
Farewel Aretus, and the souls of good men,
That as ours do, have left their Roman bodies
In brave revenge for vertue, guide our shadows,
I would not faint yet.

ARETUS
Farewel Phidias
And as we have done nobly, gods look on us.—

[Exeunt severally.

SCÆNA SECUNDA

Enter **LYCIAS**, and **PROCULUS**.

LYCIAS
Sicker, and sicker Proculus?

PROCULUS
Oh Lycias,
What shall become of us? would we had di'd
With happy Chilax, or with Balbus, bedrid—

[Enter **LICINIUS**.

And made too lame for justice.

LICINIUS
The soft Musick;
And let one sing to fasten sleep upon him:
Oh friends, the Emperour.

PROCULUS
What say the Doctors?

LICINIUS
For us a most sad saying, he is poyson'd,
Beyond all cure too.

LYCIAS
Who?

LICINIUS
The wretch Aretus,
That most unhappy villain.

LYCIAS
How do you know it?

LICINIUS
He gave him drink last: let's disperse and find him;
And since he has opened misery to all,
Let it begin with him first: Softly he slumbers.

[Enter **EMPEROUR**, sick in a Chair, with **EUDOXIA** the Empress, and **PHYSICIANS**, and **ATTENDANTS**.

[Musick and SONG.

Care charming sleep, thou easer of all woes,
Brother to death, sweetly thy self dispose
On this afflicted Prince, fall like a Cloud
In gentle showrs, give nothing that is lowd,
Or painfull to his slumbers; easie, sweet,
And as a purling stream, thou son of night,
Pass by his troubled senses; sing his pain
Like hollow murmuring wind, or silver Rain,
Into this Prince gently, Oh gently slide,
And kiss him into slumbers like a Bride.

EMPEROUR
O gods, gods: drink, drink, colder, colder
Than snow on Scythian Mountains: O my heart-strings.

EUDOXIA
How does your Grace?

PHYSICIAN
The Empress speaks Sir.

EMPEROUR
Dying,
Dying Eudoxia, dying.

PHYSICIAN
Good Sir patience.

EUDOXIA
What have ye given him?

PHYSICIAN
Pretious things dear Lady
We hope shall comfort him.

EMPEROUR
O flatter'd fool,
See what thy god-head's come to: Oh Eudoxia.

EUDOXIA
O patience, patience Sir.

[Enter **PROCULUS, LICINIUS,** with **ARETUS.**

EMPEROUR
Danubius
I'le have brought through my body.

EUDOXIA
Gods give comfort.

EMPEROUR
And Volga, on whose face the North wind freezes,
I find an hundred hells, a hundred Piles
Already to my Funerals are flaming,
Shall I not drink?

PHYSICIAN
You must not Sir.

EMPEROUR
By Heaven

I'le let my breath out that shall burn ye all
If ye deny me longer: tempests blow me,
And inundations that have drunk up Kingdoms
Flow over me, and quench me: where's the villain?
Am I immortal now ye slaves? by Numa
If he do scape: Oh, oh.

EUDOXIA
Dear Sir.

EMPEROUR
Like Nero,
But far more terrible, and full of slaughter,
I'th' midst of all my flames I'le fire the Empire:
A thousand fans, a thousand fans to cool me:
Invite the gentle winds Eudoxia.

EUDOXIA
Sir.

EMPEROUR
Oh do not flatter me, I am but flesh,
A man, a mortal man: drink, drink, ye dunces;
What can your doses now do, and your scrapings,
Your oyles, and Mithridates? if I do die,
You only words of health, and names of sickness
Finding no true disease in man but mony,
That talk your selves into Revenues, oh
And e're ye kill your patients, begger 'em,
I'le have ye flead, and dri'd.

PROCULUS
The Villain Sir;
The most accursed wretch.

EMPEROUR
Be gone my Queen,
This is no sight for thee: goe to the Vestals,
Cast holy incense in the fire, and offer
One powerfull sacrifice to free thy Cæsar.

PROCULUS
Goe goe and be happy.

[Exit **EUDOXIA**.

ARETUS
Goe, but give no ease,

The Gods have set thy last hour Valentinian,
Thou art but man, a bad man too, a beast,
And like a sensuall bloudy thing thou diest.

PROCULUS
Oh Traitor.

ARETUS
Curse your selves ye flatterers,
And howle your miseries to come ye wretches,
You taught him to be poyson'd.

EMPEROUR
Yet no comfort?

ARETUS
Be not abus'd with Priests, nor Pothecaries,
They cannot help thee; Thou hast now to live
A short half hour, no more, and I ten minutes:
I gave thee poyson for Aecius sake,
Such a destroying poyson would kill nature;
And, for thou shalt not die alone, I took it.
If mankind had been in thee at this murder,
No more to people earth again, the wings
Of old time clipt for ever, reason lost,
In what I had attempted, yet O Cæsar
To purchase fair revenge, I had poyson'd them too.

EMPEROUR
O villain: I grow hotter, hotter.

ARETUS
Yes;
But not near my heat yet; what thou feel'st now,
Mark me with horror Cæsar, are but Embers
Of lust and leachery thou hast committed:
But there be flames of murder.

EMPEROUR
Fetch out tortures.

ARETUS
Do, and I'le flatter thee, nay more I'll love thee:
Thy tortures to what now I suffer Cæsar,
At which thou must arrive too, e're thou dy'st,
Are lighter, and more full of mirth and laughter.

EMPEROUR

Let 'em alone: I must drink.

ARETUS
Now be mad,
But not near me yet.

EMPEROUR
Hold me, hold me, hold me,
Hold me; or I shall burst else.

ARETUS
See me Cæsar,
And see to what thou must come for thy murder;
Millions of womens labours, all diseases.

EMPEROUR
Oh my afflicted soul too.

ARETUS
Womens fears, horrors,
Despairs, and all the Plagues the hot Sun breeds.—

EMPEROUR
Æcius, O Aecius: O Lucina.

ARETUS
Are but my torments shadows?

EMPEROUR
Hide me mountains;
The gods have found my sins:
Now break.

ARETUS
Not yet Sir;
Thou hast a pull beyond all these.

EMPEROUR
Oh Hell,
Oh villain, cursed villain.

ARETUS
O brave villain,
My poyson dances in me at this deed:
Now Cæsar, now behold me, this is torment,
And this is thine before thou diest, I am wildfire:
The brazen Bull of Phalaris was feign'd,
The miseries of souls despising Heaven

But Emblems of my torments.

EMPEROUR
Oh quench me, quench me, quench me.

ARETUS
Fire, a flattery;
And all the Poets tales of sad Avernus,
To my pains less than fictions: Yet to shew thee
What constant love I bore my murdred master;
Like a Southwind, I have sung through all these tempests
My heart, my wither'd heart, fear, fear thou Monster,
Fear the just gods, I have my peace.—

[He dies.

EMPEROUR
More drink,
A thousand April showres fall in my bosom:
How dare ye let me be tormented thus?
Away with that prodigious body, gods,
Gods, let me ask ye what I am, ye lay
All your inflictions on me, hear me, hear me;
I do confess I am a ravisher,
A murderer, a hated Cæsar; oh,
Are there not vows enough, and flaming altars,
The fat of all the world for sacrifice,
And where that fails, the blood of thousand captives
To purge those sins? but I must make the incense?
I do despise ye all, ye have no mercy,
And wanting that, ye are no Gods, your paroll
Is only preach'd abroad to make Fools fearfull,
And women made of awe, believe your heaven:
Oh torments, torments, torments, pains above pains,
If ye be any thing but dreams, and ghosts,
And truly hold the guidance of things mortal;
Have in your selves times past, to come, and present,
Fashion the souls of men, and make flesh for 'em,
Weighing our fates, and fortunes beyond reason,
Be more than all the Gods, great in forgiveness,
Break not the goodly frame ye build in anger;
For you are things men teach us, without passions,
Give me an hour to know ye in: Oh save me
But so much perfect time ye make a soul in,
Take this destruction from me; no, ye cannot,
The more I would believe ye, more I suffer,
My brains are ashes, now my heart, my eyes friends;
I goe, I goe, more air, more air; I am mortal.—

[He dyes.

PROCULUS
Take in the body: oh Licinius,
The misery that we are left to suffer;
No pity shall find us.

LICINIUS
Our lives deserve none:
Would I were chain'd again to slavery,
With any hope of life.

PROCULUS
A quiet grave,
Or a consumption now Licinius,
That we might be too poor to kill, were something.

LICINIUS
Let's make our best use, we have mony Proculus,
And if that cannot save us, we have swords.

PROCULUS
Yes, but we dare not dye.

LICINIUS
I had forgot that:
There's other countries then.

PROCULUS
But the same hate still,
Of what we are.

LICINIUS
Think any thing, I'le follow—

[Enter a **MESSENGER**.

PROCULUS
How now, what news?

MESSENGER
Shift for your selves, ye are lost else:
The Souldier is in arms for great Aecius,
And their Lieutenant general that stopt 'em,
Cut in a thousand pieces: they march hither:
Beside, the women of the Town have murder'd
Phorba, and loose Ardelia, Cæsar's she-Bawds.

LICINIUS
Then here's no staying Proculus?

PROCULUS
O Cæsar,
That we had never known thy lusts: Let's fly,
And where we find no womans man let's dye.—

SCÆNA TERTIA

Enter **MAXIMUS**.

MAXIMUS
Gods, what a sluce of blood have I let open!
My happy ends are come to birth, he's dead,
And I reveng'd; the Empire's all a fire,
And desolation every where inhabits:
And shall I live that am the author of it,
To know Rome from the awe o'th' world, the pity?
My friends are gone before too of my sending,
And shall I stay? is ought else to be liv'd for?
Is there an other friend, another wife,
Or any third holds half their worthiness,
To linger here alive for? Is not vertue
In their two everlasting souls departed,
And in their bodies first flame fled to heaven?
Can any man discover this, and love me?
For though my justice were as white as truth,
My way was crooked to it, that condemns me:
And now Aecius, and my honored Lady,
That were preparers to my rest and quiet,
The lines to lead me to Elyzium:
You that but stept before me, on assurance
I would not leave your friendship unrewarded,
First smile upon the sacrifice I have sent ye,
Then see me coming boldly: stay, I am foolish,
Somewhat too suddain to mine own destruction,
This great end of my vengeance may grow greater:
Why may not I be Cæsar? Yet no dying;
Why should not I catch at it? fools and children
Have had that strength before me, and obtain'd it,
And as the danger stands, my reason bids me,
I will, I dare; my dear friends pardon me,
I am not fit to dye yet, if not Cæsar;
I am sure the Souldier loves me, and the people,

And I will forward, and as goodly Cedars
Rent from Oeta by a sweeping tempest
Jointed again and made tall masts, defie
Those angry winds that split 'em, so will I
New piece again, above the fate of women,
And made more perfect far, than growing private,
Stand and defie bad fortunes: If I rise,
My wife was ravish'd well; If then I fall,
My great attempt honours my Funeral.—

[Exit.

SCÆNA QUARTA

Enter **THREE SENATORS**, and **AFFRANIUS**.

1ST SENATOR
Guard all the posterns to the Camp Affranius,
And see 'em fast, we shall be rifled else,
Thou art an honest, and a worthy Captain.

2ND SENATOR
Promise the Souldier any thing.

3RD SENATOR
Speak gently,
And tell 'em we are now in council for 'em,
Labouring to choose a Cæsar fit for them,
A Souldier, and a giver.

1ST SENATOR
Tell 'em further,
Their free and liberal voices shall goe with us.

2ND SENATOR
Nay more, a negative say we allow 'em.

3RD SENATOR
And if our choice displease 'em, they shall name him.

1ST SENATOR
Promise three donatives, and large, Affranius.

2ND SENATOR
And Cæsar once elected, present foes,
With distribution of all necessaries,

Corn, Wine, and Oyle.

3RD SENATOR
New garments, and new Arms,
And equal portions of the Provinces
To them, and to their families for ever.

1ST SENATOR
And see the City strengthned.

AFFRANIUS
I shall do it.—

[Exit **AFFRANIUS**.

2ND SENATOR
Sempronius, these are wofull times.

3RD SENATOR
O Brutus,
We want thy honesty again; these Cæsars,
What noble Consuls got with blood, in blood
Consume again, and scatter.

1ST SENATOR
Which way shall we?

2ND SENATOR
Not any way of safety I can think on.

3RD SENATOR
Now go our wives to ruin, and our daughters,
And we beholders Fulvius.

1ST SENATOR
Every thing
Is every mans that will.

2ND SENATOR
The Vestals now
Must only feed the Souldiers fire of lust,
And sensual Gods be glutted with those Offerings,
Age like the hidden bowels of the earth,
Open'd with swords for treasure.
Gods defend us,
We are chaff before their fury else.

3RD SENATOR

Away,
Let's to the Temples.

1ST SENATOR
To the Capitol.
'Tis not a time to pray now, let's be strengthen'd—

[Enter **AFFRANIUS**.

3RD SENATOR
How now Affranius: what good news?

AFFRANIUS
A Cæsar.

1ST SENATOR
Oh who?

AFFRANIUS
Lord Maximus is with the Souldier,
And all the Camp rings, Cæsar, Cæsar, Cæsar:
He forced the Empress with him for more honour.

2ND SENATOR
A happy choice: let's meet him.

3RD SENATOR
Blessed fortune!

1ST SENATOR
Away, away, make room there, room there, room.

[Exeunt **SENATORS**, Flourish.

WITHIN
Lord Maximus is Cæsar, Cæsar, Cæsar;
Hail Cæsar Maximus.

AFFRANIUS
Oh turning people!
Oh people excellent in war, and govern'd,
In peace more raging than the furious North,
When he ploughs up the Sea, and makes him brine,
Or the lowd falls of Nile; I must give way,
Although I neither love nor hope this:
Or like a rotten bridge that dares a current,
When he is swell'd and high crackt, and farewel.

[Enter **MAXIMUS, EUDOXIA, SENATOR** and **SOULDIERS**.

SENATOR
Room for the Emperour.

SOULDIER
Long life to Cæsar.

AFFRANIUS
Hail Cæsar Maximus.

EMPEROUR MAXIMUS
Your hand Afranius.
Lead to the Palace, there my thanks in general,
I'le showre among ye all: gods give me life,
First to defend the Empire, then you Fathers,
And valiant friends, the heirs of strength and vertue,
The rampires of old Rome, of us the refuge;
To you I open this day all I have,
Even all the hazard that my youth hath purchas'd,
Ye are my Children, family, and friends
And ever so respected shall be, forward.
There's a Proscription, grave Sempronius,
'Gainst all the flatterers, and lazie Bawds
Led loose-liv'd Valentinian to his vices,
See it effected.

[Flourish.

SENATOR
Honour wait on Cæsar.

SOULDIER
Make room for Cæsar there.

[Exeunt all but **AFFRANIUS**.

AFFRANIUS
Thou hast my fears,
But Valentinian keeps my vows: Oh gods,
Why do we like to feed the greedy Ravenne
Of these blown men, that must before they stand,
And fixt in eminence, cast life on life,
And trench their safeties in with wounds, and bodies?
Well froward Rome, thou wilt grow weak with changing,
And die without an heir, that lov'st to breed
Sons for the killing hate of sons: for me,
I only live to find an enemy.

[Exit.

Enter **PAULUS**, a Poet, and **LICIPPUS**, a Gentleman.

PAULUS
When is the Inauguration?

LICIPPUS
Why to morrow.

PAULUS
'Twill be short time.

LICIPPUS
Any device that's handsome,
A Cupid, or the God o'th' place will do it,
Where he must take the Fasces.

PAULUS
Or a Grace.

LICIPPUS
A good Grace has no fellow.

PAULUS
Let me see,
Will not his name yield something? Maximus
By th' way of Anagram? I have found out Axis,
You know he bears the Empire.

LICIPPUS
Get him wheels too,
'Twill be a cruel carriage else.

PAULUS
Some songs too.

LICIPPUS
By any means some songs: but very short ones,
And honest language Paulus, without bursting,
The air will fall the sweeter.

PAULUS

A Grace must do it.

LICIPPUS
Why let a Grace then.

PAULUS
Yes it must be so;
And in a Robe of blew too, as I take it.

LICIPPUS
This Poet is a little kin to th' Painter
That could paint nothing but a ramping Lion,
So all his learned fancies are blew Graces.

PAULUS
What think ye of a Sea-nymph, and a Heaven?

LICIPPUS
Why what should she do there man? there's no water.

PAULUS
That's true, it must be a Grace, and yet
Me thinks a Rain bow.

LICIPPUS
And in blew.

PAULUS
Oh yes;
Hanging in arch above him, and i'th' midle—

LICIPPUS
A showre of Rain.

PAULUS
Pau. No, no, it must be a Grace.

LICIPPUS
Why prethee Grace him then.

PAULUS
Or Orpheus,
Coming from Hell.

LICIPPUS
In blew too.

PAULUS

'Tis the better;
And as he rises, full of fires.

LICIPPUS
Now bless us,
Will not that spoil his Lutestrings, Paulus?

PAULUS
Singing,
And crossing of his arms.

LICIPPUS
How can he play then?

PAULUS
It shall be a Grace, I'le do it.

LICIPPUS
Prethee do,
And with as good a grace as thou canst possible;
Good fury Paulus, be i'th' morning with me,
And pray take measure of his mouth that speaks it.

[Exeunt.

SCÆNA SEXTA

Enter **MAXIMUS** and **EUDOXIA**.

MAXIMUS
Come my best lov'd Eudoxia: let the souldier
Want neither Wine nor any thing he calls for,
And when the Senate's ready, give us notice:
In the mean time leave us.
Oh my dear sweet.

EUDOXIA
Is't possible your Grace
Should undertake such dangers for my beauty,
If it were excellent?

MAXIMUS
'Tis all
The world has left to brag of.

EUDOXIA

Can a face
Long since bequeath'd to wrinkles with my sorrows,
Long since ras'd out o'th' book of youth and pleasure,
Have power to make the strongest man o'th' Empire,
Nay the most staid, and knowing what is Woman;
The greatest aim of perfectness men liv'd by,
The most true constant lover of his wedlock,
Such a still blowing beauty, earth was proud of,
Lose such a noble wife, and wilfully;
Himself prepare the way, nay make the rape.
Did ye not tell me so?

MAXIMUS
'Tis true Eudoxia.

EUDOXIA
Lay desolate his dearest piece of friendship,
Break his strong helm he stear'd by, sink that vertue,
That valour, that even all the gods can give us,
Without whom he was nothing, with whom worthiest,
Nay more, arrive at Cæsar, and kill him too,
And for my sake? either ye love too dearly,
Or deeply ye dissemble, Sir?

MAXIMUS
I do so;
And till I am more strengthen'd, so I must do;
Yet would my joy, and Wine had fashion'd out
Some safer lye: Can these things be, Eudoxia,
And I dissemble? Can there be but goodness
And only thine dear Lady, any end,
Any imagination but a lost one,
Why I should run this hazard? O thou vertue!
Were it to do again, and Valentinian
Once more to hold thee, sinful Valentinian,
In whom thou wert set, as Pearls are in salt Oysters,
As Roses are in rank weeds, I would find,
Yet to thy sacred self a dearer danger,
The Gods know how I honour thee.

EUDOXIA
What love, Sir,
Can I return for this, but my obedience?
My life, if so you please, and 'tis too little.

MAXIMUS
'Tis too much to redeem the world.

EUDOXIA
From this hour,
The sorrows for my dead Lord, fare ye well,
My living Lord has dried ye; and in token,
As Emperour this day I honour ye,
And the great caster new of all my wishes,
The wreath of living Lawrel, that must compass
That sacred head, Eudoxia makes for Cæsar:
I am methinks too much in love with fortune;
But with you ever Royal Sir my maker,
The once more Summer of me, meer in love,
Is poor expression of my doting.

MAXIMUS
Sweetest.

EUDOXIA
Now of my troth ye have bought me dear Sir.

MAXIMUS
No,
Had I at loss of mankind.

[Enter a **MESSENGER**.

EUDOXIA
Now ye flatter.

MESSENGER
The Senate waits your Grace.

MAXIMUS
Let 'em come on,
And in a full form bring the ceremony:
This day I am your servant, dear, and proudly,
I'le wear your honoured favour.

EUDOXIA
May it prove so.

[Exeunt.

SCÆNA SEPTIMA

Enter **PAULUS** and **LICIPPUS**.

LICIPPUS
Is your Grace done?

PAULUS
'Tis done.

LICIPPUS
Who speaks?

PAULUS
A Boy.

LICIPPUS
A dainty blue Boy, Paulus?

PAULUS
Yes.

LICIPPUS
Have ye viewed
The work above?

PAULUS
Yes, and all up, and ready.

LICIPPUS
The Empress does you simple honour, Paulus,
The wreath your blue Grace must present, she made.
But hark ye, for the Souldiers?

PAULUS
That's done too:
I'le bring 'em in I warrant ye.

LICIPPUS
A Grace too?

PAULUS
The same Grace serves for both.

LICIPPUS
About it then:
I must to th' Cupbord; and be sure good Paulus
Your Grace be fasting, that he may hang cleanly.
If there should need another voice, what then?

PAULUS
I'le hang another Grace in.

LICINIUS
Grace be with ye.

[Exeunt.

SCÆNA OCTAVIA

Enter in state **MAXIMUS**, **EUDOXIA**, with **SOULDIERS** and **GENTLEMEN** of Rome, the **THREE SENATORS**, and Rods and Axes born before them.

A Synnet with Trumpets} {With a Banket prepared, with Hoboies, Musick, Song, wreath.

THIRD SENATOR
Hale to thy imperial honour sacred Cæsar,
And from the old Rome take these wishes;
You holy gods, that hitherto have held
As justice holds her Ballance equal pois'd,
This glory of our Nation, this full Roman,
And made him fit for what he is, confirm him:
Look on this Son O Jupiter our helper,
And Romulus, thou Father of our honour,
Preserve him like thy self, just, valiant, noble,
A lover, and increaser of his people,
Let him begin with Numa, stand with Cato,
The first five years of Nero be his wishes,
Give him the age and fortune of Emylius,
And his whole raign renew a great Augustus.

[**SONG**.
Honour that is ever living,
Honour that is ever giving,
Honour that sees all and knows
Both the ebbs of man and flowes,
Honour that rewards the best,
Sends thee thy rich labours rest;
Thou hast studied still to please her,
Therefore now she calls thee Cæsar:

CHORUS
Hale, hale, Cæsar, hale and stand,
And thy name outlive the Land.
Noble Fathers to his brows
Bind this wreath with thousand vows.

OMNES

Stand to Eternity.

MAXIMUS
I thank ye Fathers,
And as I rule, may it still grow or wither:
Now to the Banket, ye are all my guests,
This day be liberal friends, to wine we give it;
And smiling pleasures: Sit, my Queen of Beauty;
Fathers, your places: these are fair Wars Souldiers,
And thus I give the first charge to ye all;
You are my second, sweet, to every cup,
I add unto the Senate a new honour,
And to the sons of Mars a donative.

[**SONG.**
God Lyeus ever young,
Ever honour'd, ever sung;
Stain'd with bloud of lusty Grapes,
In a thousand lusty shapes;
Dance upon the Mazers brim,
In the Crimson liquor swim:
From thy plenteous hand divine,
Let a River run with Wine:
God of youth, let this day here
Enter neither care nor fear.

BOY
Bellona's seed, the glory of old Rome,
Envy of conquer'd Nations, nobly come
And to the fulness of your war-like noise
Let your feet move, make up this hour of joys;
Come, come I say, range your fair Troop at large,
And your high measure turn into a charge.

THIRD SENATOR
The Emperor's grown heavy with his wine.

AFFRANIUS
The Senate staies Sir for your thanks.

THIRD SENATOR
Great Cæsar.

EUDOXIA
I have my wish.

AFFRANIUS
Wilt please your Grace speak to him?

EUDOXIA
Yes, but he will not hear Lords.

THIRD SENATOR
Stir him Lucius; the Senate must have thanks.

SECOND SENATOR
Your Grace, Sir Cæsar.

EUDOXIA
Did I not tell you he was well? he's dead.

THIRD SENATOR
Dead? treason, guard the Court, let no man pass,
Souldiers, your Cæsar's murdered.

EUDOXIA
Make no tumult,
Nor arm the Court, ye have his killer with ye;
And the just cause, if ye can stay the hearing:
I was his death; that wreath that made him Cæsar,
Has made him earth.

SOULDIERS
Cut her in thousand pieces.

EUDOXIA
Wise men would know the reason first: to die,
Is that I wish for, Romans, and your swords,
The heaviest way of death: yet Souldiers grant me
That was your Empress once, and honour'd by ye,
But so much time to tell ye why I kill'd him,
And weigh my reasons well, if man be in you;
Then if ye dare do cruelly, condemn me.

AFFRANIUS
Hear her ye noble Romans, 'tis a Woman,
A subject not for swords, but pity: Heaven
(If she be guilty of malitious murder)
Has given us Laws to make example of her,
If only of revenge, and bloud hid from us,
Let us consider first, then execute.

THIRD SENATOR
Speak bloudy Woman.

EUDOXIA

Yes; This Maximus,
That was your Cæsar, Lords, and noble Souldiers,
(And if I wrong the dead, Heaven perish me;
Or speak to win your favours but the truth)
Was to his Country, to his friends, and Cæsar
A most malitious Traitor.

THIRD WOMAN
Take heed woman.

EUDOXIA
I speak not for compassion. Brave Æcius
(Whose blessed soul if I lye shall afflict me)
The man that all the world lov'd, you ador'd,
That was the master-piece of Arms, and bounty;
Mine own grief shall come last: this friend of his,
This Souldier, this your right Arm, noble Romans,
By a base letter to the Emperor;
Stufft full of fears, and poor suggestions,
And by himself, unto himself directed;
Was cut off basely, basely, cruelly;
Oh loss, O innocent, can ye now kill me?
And the poor stale my Noble Lord, that knew not
More of this villain, than his forc'd fears;
Like one foreseen to satisfie, dy'd for it:
There was a murder too, Rome would have blusht at;
Was this worth being Cæsar? or my patience? nay his Wife
By Heaven he told it me in wine, and joy;
And swore it deeply, he himself prepar'd
To be abus'd, how? let me grieve not tell ye;
And weep the sins that did it: and his end
Was only me, and Cæsar: But me he lyed in:
These are my reasons Romans, and my soul
Tells me sufficient; and my deed is justice:
Now as I have done well, or ill, look on me.

AFFRANIUS
What less could nature do, what less had we done,
Had we known this before? Romans, she is righteous;
And such a piece of justice Heaven must smile on:
Bend all your swords on me, if this displease ye.
For I must kneel, and on this vertuous hand;
Seal my new joy and thanks, thou hast done truly.

THIRD SENATOR
Up with your arms, ye strike a Saint else Romans,
May'st thou live ever spoken our Protector:
Rome yet has many Noble Heirs: Let's in

And pray, before we choose, then plant a Cæsar
Above the reach of envy, blood, and murder.

AFFRANIUS
Take up the body nobly to his urn,
And may our sins, and his together burn.

[Exeunt. A dead March.

EPILOGUE

We would fain please ye, and as fain be pleas'd;
'Tis but a little liking, both are eas'd:
We have your money, and you have our ware,
And to our understanding good and fair:
For your own wisdoms sake, be not so mad,
To acknowledge ye have bought things dear and bad:
Let not a brack i'th' Stuff, or here and there
The fading gloss, a general loss appear:
We know ye take up worse Commodities,
And dearer pay, yet think your bargains wise;
We know in Meat and Wine, ye fling away
More time and wealth, which is but dearer pay,
And with the Reckoning all the pleasure lost.
We bid ye not unto repenting cost:
The price is easie, and so light the Play,
That ye may new digest it every day.
Then noble friends, as ye would choose a Miss,
Only to please the eye a while and kiss,
Till a good Wife be got: So let this Play
Hold ye a while until a better may.

John Fletcher – A Short Biography

John Fletcher was born in December, 1579 in Rye, Sussex. He was baptised on December 20th.

As can be imagined details of much of his life and career have not survived and, accordingly, only a very brief indication of his life and works can be given.

His father, Richard Fletcher, was a successful and rather ambitious cleric. From being the Dean of Peterborough he moved on to become the Bishop of Bristol, Bishop of Worcester and finally, shortly before his death, the Bishop of London. He was also the chaplain to Queen Elizabeth.

When he was Dean of Peterborough, Richard Fletcher, witnessed the execution of Mary, Queen of Scots. It was said he "knelt down on the scaffold steps and started to pray out loud and at length, in a prolonged and rhetorical style, as though determined to force his way into the pages of history". He cried out at her death, "So perish all the Queen's enemies!" All very dramatic but the family did have strong links to the Arts.

Young Fletcher appears at the very young age of eleven to have entered Corpus Christi College at Cambridge University in 1591. There are no records that he ever took a degree but there is some small evidence that he was being prepared for a career in the church.

However what is clear is that this was soon abandoned as he joined the stream of people who would leave University and decamp to the more bohemian life of commercial theatre in London.

Unfortunately his father fell out with Queen Elizabeth but appears to have been on his way to rehabilitation before his death in 1596. At his death he was, however, mired in debt.

The upbringing of the now teenage Fletcher and his seven siblings now passed to his paternal uncle, the poet and minor official Giles Fletcher. Giles, who had the patronage of the Earl of Essex may have been a liability rather than an advantage to the young Fletcher. With Essex involved in the failed rebellion against Elizabeth Giles was also tainted by association.

By 1606 John Fletcher appears to have equipped himself with the talents to become a playwright. Initially this appears to have been for the Children of the Queen's Revels, then performing at the Blackfriars Theatre.

Commendatory verses by Richard Brome in the Beaumont and Fletcher 1647 folio place Fletcher in the company of Ben Jonson, although it is not known when this friendship began. Jonson, of course, was a leviathan of English Literature, so admired that many of his literary friends and colleagues were simply known as 'Sons of Ben'. Fletcher's frequent early collaborator, Francis Beaumont, was also a friend of Jonson's.

Fletcher's early career was marked by one significant failure; The Faithful Shepherdess, his adaptation of Giovanni Battista Guarini's Il Pastor Fido, which was performed by the Blackfriars Children in 1608. In the preface to the printed edition of his play, Fletcher explained the failure as due to his audience's faulty expectations. They expected a pastoral tragicomedy to feature dances, comedy, and murder, with the shepherds presented in conventional stereotypes – as Fletcher put it, wearing "gray cloaks, with curtailed dogs in strings." Fletcher's preface is however best known for its pithy definition of tragicomedy: "A tragicomedy is not so called in respect of mirth and killing, but in respect it wants [i.e., lacks] deaths, which is enough to make it no tragedy; yet brings some near it, which is enough to make it no comedy." A comedy, he went on to say, must be "a representation of familiar people." His preface is critical of drama that features characters whose action violates nature.

In that case, Fletcher appears to have been developing a new style faster than audiences could comprehend. By 1609, however, he had found his stride. With Beaumont, he wrote Philaster, which became a hit for the King's Men and began a profitable association between Fletcher and that company. Philaster appears also to have begun a trend for tragicomedy. Fletcher's influence has also been said to have inspired some features of Shakespeare's late romances, and certainly his influence on the tragicomic work of other playwrights is even more marked.

By the middle of the 1610s, Fletcher's plays had achieved a popularity that rivalled Shakespeare's and cemented the pre-eminence of the King's Men in Jacobean London. After Beaumont's retirement, necessitated by ill-health, and then his early death in 1616, Fletcher continued working, both singly and in collaboration, until his death in 1625. By that time, he had produced, or had been credited with, close to fifty plays. This body of work remained a major part of the King's Men's repertory until the closing of the theatres in 1642 due to the Civil War.

At the beginning of his career Fletcher's most important collaborator was Francis Beaumont. The two wrote together for close to a decade, first for the Children of the Queen's Revels, and then for the King's Men. According to an anecdote transmitted or invented by John Aubrey, they also lived together in Bankside, sharing clothes and having "one wench in the house between them." This domestic arrangement, if it existed, was ended by Beaumont's marriage in 1613, and their dramatic partnership ended after Beaumont fell ill, probably of a stroke, that same year.

At this point Fletcher had written many plays with Beaumont and several others on his own. He seems to have been regarded as quite a talent although it should be remembered that playwrights were required to be prolific, to easily work with other collaborators and to produce work of quality and commercial appeal very quickly.

The King's Men, run by Philip Henslowe, was the most prestigious of the theatre companies and Fletcher now had an increasingly close association with it.

Fletcher collaborated with Shakespeare on Henry VIII, The Two Noble Kinsmen, and the now lost Cardenio, which some scholars say was the basis for Lewis Theobald's play Double Falsehood. (Theobald is regarded as one of the best Shakespearean editors. Whether his play is based on Cardenio or on some other is not absolutely known although Theobald certainly promoted it as his revision of the lost Shakespeare/Fletcher play.)

A play that Fletcher also wrote by himself at this time, The Woman's Prize or the Tamer Tamed, is also regarded as a sequel to The Taming of the Shrew.

In 1616, with the death of Shakespeare, Fletcher now appears to have entered into an enhanced arrangement with the King's Men on very similar terms to Shakespeare's. Fletcher would now write exclusively for the King's Men until his own death almost a decade later.

As well as continuing his solo productions Fletcher was still collaborating with other playwrights, mainly Philip Massinger, who, in turn, would succeed him as the in-house playwright for the King's Men.

Fletcher's popularity continued throughout his life; indeed during the winter of 1621, he had three of his plays performed at court. His mastery is most notable in two dramatic types; tragicomedy and the comedy of manners.

John Fletcher died in 1625, it is thought of bubonic plague which, at the time, was undergoing further outbreaks.

He seems to have been buried in what is now Southwark Cathedral, although a precise location is not known. There is much made of an anecdote that Fletcher and Massinger (who died in 1640) share the same grave but it is more likely that both are buried within a few yards of each other and that the stone markers in the floor have confused the issue. One is marked 'Edmond Shakespeare 1607' and the other 'John Fletcher 1625' refers to Shakespeare's younger brother and the playwright. The churchyards were, more often than not, completely over-crowded and breeding grounds for disease. Precise record keeping was not a practiced skill.

During the later Commonwealth, many of the playwright's best-known scenes were kept alive as drolls. These were brief performances, usually condensed into one or two scenes and with the addition of music or song to satisfy the taste for plays while the theatres were closed under the Puritans. At the re-opening of the theatres in 1660, the plays in the Fletcher canon, in original form or revised, were by far the most common productions on the English stage. The most frequently revived plays suggest the developing taste for comedies of manners. Among the tragedies, The Maid's Tragedy and, especially, Rollo Duke of Normandy held the stage. Four tragicomedies (A King and No King, The Humorous Lieutenant, Philaster, and The Island Princess) were popular, perhaps in part for their similarity to and foreshadowing of heroic drama. Four comedies (Rule a Wife And Have a Wife, The Chances, Beggars' Bush, and especially The Scornful Lady) were also stage mainstays.

Despite his popularity, and it appears he was held in higher regard than Shakespeare at this time, his works steadily lost ground to those of Shakespeare and to new productions from other playwrights.

Since then Fletcher has increasingly become a subject only for occasional revivals and for specialists. Fletcher and his collaborators have been the subject of important bibliographic and critical studies, but the plays have been revived only infrequently.

Due to the frequent collaborations between all manner of playwrights, and the revisions carried out in later years, having a settled list of authorship to any given set of plays can be problematic. The works of Fletcher and others of this period most definitely fall into this category. It is as well to take into account that during this period theatres were quite often closed either due to outbreaks of the plague or to the prevailing political and moral climate. Printers, anxious to provide materials that would sell, were not above changing a name or two to enhance sales.

Although Fletcher collaborated most often with Beaumont and Massinger, it is believed that Massinger revised many of the plays some time after their original production. Other collaborators including Nathan Field, William Shakespeare, William Rowley and others also can be seen distinctly in Fletchers' works. Many modern scholars point out that Fletcher had many particular mannerisms but other playwrights would also duplicate these at times so allocating exact contributions of anyone to a play is somewhat of a detective case in many instances. However from the original folio printings or licensing via the Master of the Revels (the statutory licensing authority to approve and censor plays as well a hand in publication and printing of theatrical materials) as well as contemporary notes a fairly precise bibliography of the works can be given with only a few plays lacking substantial authority and provenance.

John Fletcher – A Concise Bibliography

This bibliography gives the most likely date of writing together with when published, revised or licensed by the Master or the Revels (This position within the royal household was originally for royal festivities, ie revels, and later to oversee stage censorship, until this function was transferred to the Lord Chamberlain in 1624).

Solo Plays
The Faithful Shepherdess, pastoral (written 1608–9; printed 1609)
The Tragedy of Valentinian, tragedy (1610–14; 1647)
Monsieur Thomas, comedy (c. 1610–16; 1639)
The Woman's Prize, or The Tamer Tamed, comedy (c. 1611; 1647)
Bonduca, tragedy (1611–14; 1647)
The Chances, comedy (c. 1613–25; 1647)
Wit Without Money, comedy (c. 1614; 1639)
The Mad Lover, tragicomedy (acted 5 January 1617; 1647)
The Loyal Subject, tragicomedy (licensed 16 November 1618; revised 1633; 1647)
The Humorous Lieutenant, tragicomedy (c. 1619; 1647)
Women Pleased, tragicomedy (c. 1619–23; 1647)
The Island Princess, tragicomedy (c. 1620; 1647)
The Wild Goose Chase, comedy (c. 1621; 1652)
The Pilgrim, comedy (c. 1621; 1647)
A Wife for a Month, tragicomedy (licensed 27 May 1624; 1647)
Rule a Wife and Have a Wife, comedy (licensed 19 October 1624; 1640)

Collaborations

With Francis Beaumont
The Woman Hater, comedy (1606; 1607)
Cupid's Revenge, tragedy (c. 1607–12; 1615)
Philaster, or Love Lies a-Bleeding, tragicomedy (c. 1609; 1620)
The Maid's Tragedy, Tragedy (c. 1609; 1619)
A King and No King, tragicomedy (1611; 1619)
The Captain, comedy (c. 1609–12; 1647)
The Scornful Lady, comedy (c. 1613; 1616)
Love's Pilgrimage, tragicomedy (c. 1615–16; 1647)
The Noble Gentleman, comedy (c. 1613; licensed 3 February 1626; 1647)

With Francis Beaumont & Philip Massinger
Thierry & Theodoret, tragedy (c. 1607; 1621)
The Coxcomb, comedy (c. 1608–10; 1647)
Beggars' Bush, comedy (c. 1612–13; revised 1622; 1647)
Love's Cure, comedy (c. 1612–13; revised 1625; 1647)

With Philip Massinger
Sir John van Olden Barnavelt, tragedy (August 1619; MS)
The Little French Lawyer, comedy (c. 1619–23; 1647)
A Very Woman, tragicomedy (c. 1619–22; licensed 6 June 1634; 1655)
The Custom of the Country, comedy (c. 1619–23; 1647)
The Double Marriage, tragedy (c. 1619–23; 1647)
The False One, history (c. 1619–23; 1647)

The Prophetess, tragicomedy (licensed 14 May 1622; 1647)
The Sea Voyage, comedy (licensed 22 June 1622; 1647)
The Spanish Curate, comedy (licensed 24 October 1622; 1647)
The Lovers' Progress or The Wandering Lovers, tragicomedy (licensed 6 December 1623; rev 1634; 1647)
The Elder Brother, comedy (c. 1625; 1637)

With Philip Massinger & Nathan Field
The Honest Man's Fortune, tragicomedy (1613; 1647)
The Queen of Corinth, tragicomedy (c. 1616–18; 1647)
The Knight of Malta, tragicomedy (c. 1619; 1647)

With William Shakespeare
Henry VIII, history (c. 1613; 1623)
The Two Noble Kinsmen, tragicomedy (c. 1613; 1634)
Cardenio, tragicomedy (c. 1613)

With Thomas Middleton & William Rowley
Wit at Several Weapons, comedy (c. 1610–20; 1647)

With William Rowley
The Maid in the Mill (licensed 29 August 1623; 1647).

With Nathan Field
Four Plays, or Moral Representations, in One, morality (c. 1608–13; 1647)

With Philip Massinger, Ben Jonson and George Chapman
Rollo Duke of Normandy, or The Bloody Brother, tragedy (c. 1617; revised 1627–30; 1639)

With James Shirley
The Night Walker, or The Little Thief, comedy (c. 1611; 1640)
The Coronation c. 1635

Uncertain
The Nice Valour, or The Passionate Madman, comedy (c. 1615–25; 1647)
The Laws of Candy, tragicomedy (c. 1619–23; 1647)
The Fair Maid of the Inn, comedy (licensed 22 January 1626; 1647)
The Faithful Friends, tragicomedy (registered 29 June 1660; MS.)

The Nice Valour is possibly by Fletcher revised by Thomas Middleton;

The Fair Maid of the Inn is perhaps a play by Massinger, John Ford, and John Webster, either with or without Fletcher's involvement.

The Laws of Candy has been variously attributed to Fletcher and to John Ford.

The Night-Walker was a Fletcher original, with additions by Shirley for a 1639 production.

Even now there is not absolute certainty on several of the plays. The first Beaumont & Fletcher folio of 1647 contained 35 plays and the second folio of 1679 added a further 18. In total 53 plays.

The first folio included The Masque of the Inner Temple and Gray's Inn (1613), and the second The Knight of the Burning Pestle (1607), widely considered Beaumont's solo works, although the latter was in early editions attributed to both writers. Fletcher himself said that Beaumont was attributed so-authorship of many works that belonged solely to Fletcher or to other collaborators.

One play in the canon, Sir John Van Olden Barnavelt, existed in manuscript and was not published till 1883.

www.ingramcontent.com/pod-product-compliance
Lightning Source LLC
Chambersburg PA
CBHW060313050426
42448CB00009B/1816